Non-Profit Creation

And Management

Jonathan & Donna Vorce

Jonathan Vorce Ministries, Inc.

Non-Profit Creation and Management

Copyright © 2024 by Jonathan Vorce

All rights reserved.

First Edition: 2024

Scripture quotations taken from:

The Holy Bible, New International Version® NIV®

Copyright © 1973, 1978, 1984, 2011 by Biblica, Inc.

Used with permission. All rights reserved worldwide.

The Holy Bible, English Standard Version ® ESV

Copyright © 2001 by Crossway, a publishing ministry of Good News Publishers. Used by permission.

The New King James Version® NKJV®

Scripture taken from the New King James Version®. Copyright © 1982 by Thomas Nelson. Used by permission. All rights reserved.

King James Version (KJV), public domain.

No part of this book may be reproduced, scanned, or distributed in any printed or electronic form without permission. Please do not participate in or encourage piracy of copyrighted materials in violation of the author's rights. Thank you for respecting the hard work of this author.

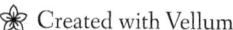 Created with Vellum

Contents

Introduction   v

1. An Overview of Non-Profit Organizations   1
2. Non-Profit Evolution   11
3. The Legal Evolution of Non-Profits   21
4. Setting up a Non-Profit   31
5. Raising Capital   43
6. Non-Profit Finances   57
7. Mastering the Art of Non-Profit Board Meetings   73
8. Non-Profit Management Styles   85
9. HR Strategies for Faith-Based Organizations   93
10. The Path to Non-Profit Sustainability   107

May I Introduce You to Jesus?   135
About the Author   143
Also by Jonathan & Donna Vorce   145

Introduction

For several decades, my spouse, Donna, and I have engaged in the foundation and management of various initiatives categorized under Non-Profit Ministries. Our initial foray into this sector involved personally navigating the procedures for acquiring non-profit certifications from the Internal Revenue Service (IRS) for our own ministry endeavors. Over time, this experience has positioned us as a resource for others seeking guidance on establishing their own non-profit entities. Common inquiries we encounter pertain to the foundational steps for setting up a non-profit like, the development of Articles of Incorporation, assistance in drafting Constitutions and By-Laws, and setting up a Launch Plan.

Additionally, we have had the honor of imparting knowledge on several non-profit management subjects including, but not limited to, how to organize and run a board room, implementing the motions passed in the real world, and strategies to secure funding for approved projects.

This book serves as an introductory guide to these subjects, and more, providing historical context on non-profit organiza-

Introduction

tions, straightforward responses to prevalent questions, and supplementary insights that may benefit readers interested in pursuing non-profit endeavors. It is our sincere hope that this resource empowers you to achieve successful and effective results in your mission to serve others.

Jonathan & Donna

Chapter 1

An Overview of Non-Profit Organizations

In contemporary society, financial achievement is frequently the benchmark for success. However, within this paradigm exists a distinct sector that deviates from the norm—non-profit organizations. These entities are integral to the societal framework, epitomizing a business model founded on altruism rather than profit maximization.[*]

Non-profit organizations differ fundamentally from for-profit entities in their core mission and operational ethos. While for-profit businesses aim to maximize profits for their shareholders, non-profits seek to address specific societal needs or advocate for particular causes without the primary objective of financial gain. This divergence in foundational purpose significantly influences their approach to governance, funding, and stakeholder engagement.[†]

The governance structure of non-profits typically involves a board of directors or trustees who oversee the organization's

---

[*] "Defining the Nonprofit Sector," Stanford Social Innovation Review, 2022
[†] "Non-Profit vs For-Profit Organizations," Harvard Business Review, 2021

operations, ensuring adherence to its mission and responsible management of resources. Funding for non-profits often relies on donations, grants, and volunteer services, contrasting with for-profit entities that depend on revenue generated from products or services.*

Furthermore, non-profit organizations play a pivotal role in providing essential services, advocating for social change, and enhancing community well-being. Their contribution extends beyond immediate service delivery, influencing public policy and societal norms through advocacy and awareness-raising activities.†

Therefore, non-profit organizations embody a business model that prioritizes societal benefit over financial profit. This unique orientation not only differentiates them from their for-profit counterparts but also amplifies their impact on social welfare and community development.

Defining the Non-Profit Ethos

Non-profit organizations, also known as NGOs (non-governmental organizations), embody a commitment to advancing public welfare. Their foundational purpose is to enhance societal well-being, contrasting sharply with the profit-centric motive of their for-profit counterparts. This commitment is evident in their operational model, which prioritizes the reinvestment of any financial surplus into their primary mission, rather than distributing profits to shareholders.

These entities cover a broad spectrum of causes and sectors, from local grassroots movements to globally recognized

---

* "Governance and Funding of Non-Profit Organizations," Nonprofit Quarterly, 2020
† "The Role of Nonprofits in Society," Journal of Public Policy & Marketing, 2023

charities to local houses of worship. Their areas of focus include but are not limited to healthcare, education, churches, environmental preservation, and human rights advocacy. Despite the diversity of their missions, non-profits are united by a core ethos: a dedication to societal and spiritual improvement executed with integrity and transparency.

The financial practices of non-profit organizations are governed by the principle of stewardship. This approach ensures that resources are utilized judiciously, with a keen focus on maximizing impact rather than generating financial gain. Such an ethos is critical in maintaining the trust and support of donors, volunteers, and the communities they serve.

The significance of non-profits in the global fabric cannot be overstated. They address gaps in services and advocacy that neither the private sector nor government agencies fully cover. Through their dedicated work, non-profits not only provide immediate assistance and relief but also champion long-term solutions to systemic issues. Their role in advocating for policy changes, raising awareness, and mobilizing resources has a profound effect on societal progress and equity.

Finally, the non-profit ethos is characterized by a steadfast commitment to public good, operationalized through transparent, ethical practices and a financial model centered on mission over profit. This unique approach enables non-profit organizations to make a significant, lasting impact on a wide array of social, environmental, spiritual, and economic challenges.

The Integral Role in Society

Society faces numerous challenges, ranging from social injustices to environmental crises. In addressing these issues, the unique contributions of non-profit organizations are invaluable. Unlike public agencies, which may be constrained by bureaucratic procedures, non-profits offer a distinct advantage due to their agility, purpose-driven missions, and relentless commitment to service.

Non-profits act not as substitutes for government institutions but as essential partners, enhancing the capabilities of public agencies through their flexibility. This adaptability enables them to respond swiftly to sudden crises and devise innovative approaches to longstanding societal problems.

A critical function of non-profit organizations is to serve as advocates for marginalized groups. They give voice to those who might otherwise be unheard, championing causes related to justice and equity. Through their efforts, non-profits play a pivotal role in pushing for systemic change, influencing policy, and raising public awareness on key issues.

Non-profits frequently act as the cornerstone of support in many communities, bridging the voids neglected by the public and private sectors. From offering vital services like healthcare and education to championing environmental preservation and human rights, or providing welfare rooted in faith, these organizations often emerge as critical lifelines for both individuals and entire communities. Their efforts span a wide array of needs, guaranteeing that no one is left behind.

Non-profit organizations occupy a critical space within society's ecosystem. By leveraging their unique strengths—agility, purposefulness, and a deep-seated drive to serve—they complement the efforts of public agencies while filling vital roles that neither government nor business adequately cover. Their dedication to serving as voices for the marginalized and acting as key providers of essential services underscores the indispensable role they play in fostering a more just and equitable society.

Cultivating a Community of Believers

The non-profit sector is characterized by a dynamic and expansive ecosystem that encompasses more than just the organizations at its core. This vibrant community is supported by a diverse array of contributors, including churches, faith-based and para-church ministries, communities, donors, supporters, and volunteers. It is the collective faith and commitment of these groups that enable non-profit organizations to transform aspirational goals into concrete outcomes.

Volunteers play a crucial role within this ecosystem, acting as the operational arms that carry out the benevolent activities of these organizations. Similarly, donors represent the foundational support, providing the necessary resources that sustain the operations and initiatives of non-profits. Together, these elements contribute to the vitality and sustainability of the non-profit sector.

The appeal of engaging with non-profit organizations extends beyond simple acts of philanthropy. It involves a deeper integration of one's personal and professional life with a mission that serves a greater purpose. Choosing a career path in the non-profit realm is often driven by a sense of vocation—an expression of one's faith through practical action. This decision is not taken lightly; it embodies a profound dedication to making a meaningful difference in the world.

In essence, the non-profit sector thrives on the collective efforts of individuals and groups who are motivated by a shared vision of societal improvement. Their contribution is not just a matter of performing tasks; it is an act of faith, a testament to their belief in the power of collective action to effect positive change. The sector's ability to realize its objectives is deeply rooted in this community of believers, whose participation is essential for turning visions of impact into palpable realities.

Tax Benefits

In the realm of non-profits, financial management and tax exemption policies are critical considerations. The provision of tax benefits to non-profit organizations is a significant legislative measure, serving as a formal acknowledgment and support of their contributions to society. This policy is not merely a fiscal strategy; it symbolizes a mutual recognition between the state and non-profits of the valuable work being conducted outside the governmental purview.

For these organizations, the advantages of tax-exempt status are substantial. It allows for a greater proportion of their funds to be allocated directly towards their missions and projects. This optimization of resources enhances the efficacy and reach of their initiatives, thereby maximizing societal impact. The tax benefits bestowed upon non-profits can be seen as the government's way of facilitating and encouraging their activities, essentially acting as an endorsement of their efforts to address various social, environmental, and cultural issues.

This arrangement creates a symbiotic relationship between the government and non-profit sector. On one hand, the government acknowledges the crucial role of non-profits in filling gaps in public services and addressing needs that fall beyond the scope of its direct action. On the other, non-profits benefit from a more favorable economic environment, which allows them to extend their services and amplify their impact on the community.

The implications of this dynamic are profound. Society at large benefits from a more robust and vibrant public service sector, enriched by the diverse and specialized contributions of non-profit organizations. These tax provisions, therefore, play a pivotal role in fostering a conducive environment for non-profits to thrive, thereby enhancing their capacity to serve as vital agents of social change.

In summary, tax benefits for non-profits represent a key element in the broader financial ecosystem that supports their operations. This legislative support is crucial, not only for the sustainability of non-profits but also for the vitality of the public service sector and the overall well-being of society.

How One Can Integrate Business and Ministry

The non-profit sector presents a unique opportunity for businesses, individuals, and members of the clergy to blend their entrepreneurial skills with the deeply rooted service ethos of ministry. This integration allows for the creation of non-profit ministries that leverage both business acumen and commitment to service, facilitating impactful social change.

One of the most effective ways to achieve this blend is through mentorship. Established professionals can guide emerging non-profits, imparting valuable business insights and strategies that enhance the organization's efficiency and impact. Mentorship not only aids in capacity building but also fosters a culture of learning and collaboration within the non-profit sector.

Strategic investment is another crucial element. By allocating resources—be it financial, human, or technical—businesses and individuals can support the growth of non-profit ministries. Investments help these organizations scale their operations, extend their reach, and increase their societal impact. This approach demonstrates a tangible commitment to the non-profit's mission, bolstering its effectiveness and sustainability.

Partnerships represent a powerful mechanism for crossing sectoral boundaries, uniting the non-profit and for-profit worlds in a common cause. Such collaborations allow for the sharing of expertise, resources, and networks, creating synergies that amplify the work of non-profit ministries. These partnerships can take various forms, from joint initiatives and project sponsorships to shared resource platforms, each contributing to a deeper, more meaningful engagement with societal challenges.

The convergence of business and ministry within the non-profit ecosystem encourages a holistic approach to addressing societal needs. It underscores the idea that contributions to the greater good are not limited by vocational boundaries. Rather, it highlights the potential for collective action to achieve outcomes that are indeed greater than the sum of individual efforts.

The integration of business acumen and ministry ethos in the non-profit sector opens avenues for innovative approaches to social change. Through mentorship, strategic investment, and cross-sector partnerships, a more inclusive, collaborative, and impactful model of non-profit ministry can be realized, inviting participation from all sectors of society.

The Role of NPO's in Enhancing Human Society

The annals of human history are replete with stories that highlight a deep-seated altruism at the heart of society. In this vast tapestry, the non-profit organization shines brightly, exemplifying collective human kindness and selfless efforts. These entities are the bedrock on which societies anchor their hopes and strive for loftier values. They epitomize the spirit of service, seamlessly blending the sacred with the secular to form a unified whole. This amalgamation lifts the notion of service beyond mere obligation, transforming it into an act that borders on the sacred.

Non-Profit Creation

Non-profit organizations offer a unique platform for individuals who are already contributing within this sector or those seeking to engage in meaningful participation. This invitation is not merely to observe but to become integral components of this vibrant ecosystem. The amalgamation of individual efforts within the non-profit sector promises the transformation of individual lives, the enhancement of community well-being, and the upliftment of our collective existential experience.

The current moment presents an opportune time for individuals and businesses to bridge the gap between commerce and ministry through involvement in the non-profit sector. This integration is not only commendable but aligns with a higher purpose, that of pleasing God. Such endeavors contribute significantly to bringing a semblance of the blessing into our earthly existence, enriching the very fabric of human society.

In conclusion, the narrative of non-profit organizations is a powerful testament to the capacity for collective human action to effect positive change. Through the strategic integration of business principles with the ethos of ministry, non-profits stand as pivotal entities in our pursuit of a more equitable and compassionate world. Their contribution transcends mere service, touching heaven and uplifting humanity in profound ways.

Chapter 2

Non-Profit Evolution

Throughout history, non-profit organizations and ministries have been pivotal in driving social change. Their role, deeply entwined within the fabric of our communities, has been instrumental from the earliest societies to the present day. These entities work hand in hand with governments and businesses, playing a critical role in tackling and improving societal issues. But what we're looking into here is not merely a recounting of their past; it's an in-depth exploration of how these organizations have evolved, their current state, and their potential future impact.

Why focus on this sector? Because understanding the significant and dynamic role of non-profits and ministries can empower us to see beyond their activities to the heart of their mission. This exploration offers a chance to deepen one's appreciation for the dedication and broad-reaching effects these organizations, and the people who run them, have worldwide.

Historical Context

Have you ever paused to consider the profound legacy of non-profit organizations and ministries? Their roots stretch deep into the annals of history, back to the ancient civilizations that laid the groundwork for a tradition of charity and compassion. Imagine societies in Mesopotamia, Greece, and Rome, where the foundations of support for the less fortunate were laid, not just by the government, but through the heartfelt generosity of individuals and the guiding principles of religious institutions.

- In Ancient Mesopotamia, as far back as 4000 BCE, the world witnessed one of its earliest forms of organized charity. The Sumerians introduced the concept of communal support, establishing funds within temple communities to aid the poor, the sick, and those in need.
- Fast forward to Ancient Greece around 500 BCE, where the notion of philanthropy began to take shape, with the wealthy patrons of Athens supporting public works, and providing for the less fortunate, essentially laying the groundwork for modern philanthropy.
- Meanwhile, Ancient Rome, around 27 BCE - 476 CE, further developed the concept of benevolence by instituting formal systems of social welfare. These included the annona, a state-run grain distribution to ensure the poor could eat, and the alimenta, funds to support the upbringing and education of children.

These historical examples not only illustrate the deep-seated tradition of charity within human societies but also showcase the enduring human spirit of generosity that transcends time and geography, setting the stage for the non-profit entities and ministries that flourish today.

Isn't it remarkable how the threads of charity and care woven by early Christian and Jewish communities have evolved into the complex tapestry of today's non-profit sector? These texts are not merely historical records; they are testimonies to a legacy of caring for those in need—widows, orphans, and the marginalized. They highlight how the values of compassion and giving have been institutionalized over millennia, serving as the bedrock for the modern-day non-profit movement.

The spirit of charity and community care exhibited by the Jewish people and early Christians forms a vital part of the mosaic that is today's charitable landscape.

- **Jewish Philanthropy**: Historically, Jewish law incorporated the concept of 'tzedakah', a form of charity that goes beyond mere giving. It is considered a moral obligation to support those in need, ensuring the well-being of the community. From as early as the 1st century, Jewish communities established a communal fund for the poor, known as the 'kuppah', which was distributed regularly. Additionally, the 'tamchui', a communal kitchen, provided food for the hungry on a daily basis. This system of structured charity reflects a deep-rooted belief in collective responsibility toward societal welfare, a principle that remains at the core of many modern non-profit organizations.

- **Early Christian Charity**: The early Christian communities, following the teachings of Jesus, placed a great emphasis on care for the poor, sick, and marginalized. The Book of Acts in the New Testament (circa 1st century AD) portrays the first Christians in Jerusalem as living communally, sharing their possessions, and ensuring none among them suffered need (Acts 4:32-35). This practice of sharing and mutual aid became a hallmark of Christian communities. Around the 3rd century, the Christian church formalized the role of the 'diaconate' to oversee the distribution of aid to the poor, an early example of organized charity that laid the groundwork for the development of Christian ministries dedicated to social welfare and community support.

These historical examples from Jewish and early Christian communities further underscore a shared commitment to fostering societies that care for the less fortunate. This legacy of benevolence and communal support has profoundly influenced the development of charitable ministries throughout history, positioning them as foundational pillars in the construction of the comprehensive, global network of non-profit organizations we see today.

The Role of Industrialization

Have you ever stopped to ponder the monumental shifts that the 18th and 19th centuries brought to our world? It was a time when the landscape of society was forever altered by the forces of industrialization, sparking not just technological advancements but also reshaping the human story. With cities expanding at an unprecedented pace, the dark underbelly of progress revealed itself in the form of slums and the harrowing living conditions endured by the urban poor. However,

> "Where there is great need, there is also great opportunity for compassion and action."

Isn't it awe-inspiring how, in the face of such adversity, both religious and secular communities rallied together, evolving more systematic approaches to tackle these emerging social challenges? This era wasn't just about the rise of industry; it was about the birth of a more formalized effort to care for our fellow beings.

Consider the United Way in the United States, established with a noble mission to promote *"the common good."* Or take the founding of the Society for the Prevention of Cruelty to Animals (SPCA) in England, a beacon for animal welfare non-profits worldwide. What about the Salvation Army? Founded in England in the mid-19th century, it quickly spread across Europe and North America, providing food, shelter, and spiritual support to those most in need. These weren't mere organizational births; they were declarations that in the march towards progress, no individual, no creature should be left behind.

It's clear that industrialization did more than just transform economies and landscapes; it served as a powerful catalyst for the evolution of non-profit organizations. But why does this matter to us today? Why should we, standing at the intersection of business and ministry, take a moment to reflect on this chapter of history?

Why Us... Why Now?

Now, why does this matter to us today? Why should we, as individuals navigating the crossroads of business and ministry in our lives, take a moment to reflect on this history? It's simple. This rich heritage embodies the essence of what it means to serve—to live out a calling that transcends the mere pursuit of personal success and ventures into the realm of making a tangible difference in the world.

We are presented with an invitation—an opportunity to unlock our potential not just as professionals but as compassionate humans called to serve. How can we, in our daily lives and work, carry forward the legacy of those who rose to meet the needs of their time with courage and innovation?

This isn't just about looking back; it's about moving forward with purpose, driven by the knowledge that every challenge we face is an opportunity to live out our faith through service. This is our call to action—a rallying cry for those eager to blend their professional endeavors with their spiritual missions. Imagine the possibilities when the wealth of your knowledge and the depth of your faith converge to create lasting change.

Look at it this way, we are offered a pathway to empowerment. A way to create a sense of belonging among all who dare to dream of a better world. Through understanding our shared history and its connection to the present, we can unlock the full potential within each of us to make a difference.

The Impact of Non-Profits

Have you paused to consider the monumental impact non-profits have on our world? It's a realm where passion meets purpose, and the results are nothing short of miraculous. From responding to disasters with speed and compassion, to alleviating suffering in local communities through faith-based initiatives, the spectrum of challenges tackled by non-profits is a testament to their incredible versatility and indomitable spirit.

But what truly sets non-profits apart? Is it their unwavering commitment to social movements, their historic role in championing fundamental changes such as civil rights, women's suffrage, and healthcare reform? Indeed, these organizations are not just participants in the narrative of change; they are the architects, the visionaries who dare to imagine a better world.

Consider the sheer power of a non-profit to mobilize resources, elevate public awareness, and spur grassroots activism. It's a dynamic force, sculpting the future one cause at a time. And isn't it fascinating how comparative analyses show that nations flourishing with robust non-profit sectors enjoy higher levels of social welfare and civic engagement?

This brings us to an invigorating reflection:

> "What if we harnessed this power, blending the realms of business and ministry to ignite a revolution of compassion and transformation?"

By understanding the pillars upon which non-profits stand and the unparalleled impact they have forged, we unlock the full spectrum of our capacity to contribute. Together, we can transform challenges into opportunities for growth, innovation, and heartfelt service in every corner of the globe. Speaking of "across the globe..."

Global Development

Consider for a moment the stark contrasts and vibrant similarities in non-profit development across different countries—each narrative is as distinct as the land itself. Developed nations often showcase expansive non-profit sectors, broad in scope and deep in influence. Here, organizations flourish, propelled by a combination of robust economies and a culture of philanthropy. Isn't it inspiring to see such powerful engines of change?

Now, turn your gaze to the emerging economies, where non-profits are witnessing unprecedented growth. Amidst social and economic upheaval, these organizations emerge as beacons of hope, rooted in grassroots efforts to uplift and empower. Their work is not just about providing services; it's a clarion call for societal transformation, one life at a time. Can you feel the pulse of potential in these vibrant movements?

Take, for example, the Scandinavian countries, where the welfare state has historically intertwined with a dynamic non-profit sector. This synergy not only reinforces social cohesion but also weaves a safety net that reduces dependence on government services. What if we could draw lessons from this model, weaving together the fibers of community support and national welfare with grace and efficiency?

In contrast, developing nations offer a canvas where non-profits paint hope with broad strokes. These organizations are often grassroots-oriented, their work embedded in the very fabric of the communities they serve. They strive to provide basic services, yes, but their vision extends far beyond—it's about empowering the marginalized, giving voice to the voiceless. Isn't this the essence of ministry, the very heart of service?

Why does this matter, you might ask? Why should we, as individuals blessed with the fusion of faith and profession, immerse ourselves in this global narrative? Because understanding the multifaceted development of non-profits around the world isn't just about acknowledging diversity—it's about recognizing our shared humanity and our collective call to serve. We really are together in this experience called life!

The Future of Non-Profits

The path ahead for non-profits is one of innovation and adaptability. Can you imagine the incredible potential that lies in harnessing rapid technological advances, demographic shifts, and our growing global interconnectedness? This is not just about surviving; it's about thriving, transforming, and reaching new heights of impact.

But what does sustainability look like in this dynamic landscape? It rests on the pillars of innovation, collaboration, and relevance. The future demands that non-profits not only keep pace with evolving priorities and donor expectations but also lead the way in creating meaningful change. Have you seen how digital platforms and social media are already rewriting the playbook for stakeholder engagement and fundraising? This is just the beginning.

Why does this matter, you ask? Why should we, standing at the intersection of business and ministry, pay heed to these shifts? Because now, more than ever, we are called to unlock our potential, to blend our professional expertise with our spiritual mission.

Together, we stand on the brink of a new era for non-profits, armed with the power of faith, innovation, and shared purpose. This isn't just an invitation; it's a pathway to empowerment, a call to live out our calling with renewed passion and determination.

By understanding the shifting sands beneath our feet, we can chart a course that not only navigates but transcends the challenges ahead. Together, we can transform the future of non-profits into a beacon of hope, innovation, and enduring impact.

The evolution of non-profits is a testament to the enduring human drive for compassion and social responsibility. From humble roots in ancient times to the global entities of today, non-profits have traversed a remarkable path, leaving an indelible mark on the world they seek to improve. As we stand at the cusp of a new era, the narrative of non-profits is being rewritten by a new generation of leaders and activists who are committed to confronting the challenges of tomorrow with the same spirit of service that has characterized the sector from its inception.

A deep understanding of this evolution is not just an academic exercise; it is a roadmap for designing impactful programs, advocating for change, and creating a legacy of social transformation. The future belongs to those who can envision it, and through the lens of non-profits, we see a future filled with potential, promise, and a resolute commitment to the public good.

Chapter 3

The Legal Evolution of Non-Profits

Imagine the early 20th century, a pivotal era when the concept of non-governmental organizations (NGOs) began to crystallize in the legal realm. Have you considered what it meant for an organization to be granted 'charitable immunity'? This legal doctrine was a turning point, offering a shield against baseless claims that could potentially derail their benevolent initiatives. Isn't it remarkable how the law began to recognize the intrinsic value of these missions, fostering an environment where they could thrive without undue hindrance?

Now, cast your mind back even further to the Charitable Uses Act of 1601 in England, a landmark moment that propelled the formal recognition of non-profits into motion. Fast forward to the Tax Reform Act of 1969 in the United States, and we witness another leap forward in solidifying the distinct advantages and responsibilities of non-profit entities. These legislative milestones didn't just redefine the operational landscape; they amplified the capacity of non-profits to make a difference through enhanced fundraising abilities, tax-exempt status, and the execution of diverse programs and services within the bounds of the law.

But why is this legal evolution so crucial for us today? Why should we, standing at the intersection of commerce and compassion, reflect upon these milestones? It's because understanding this legal heritage empowers us to harness our collective potential not merely as bystanders but as active participants in this legacy of change.

The Evolution of NPO's in the United States

The United States, with its robust history of volunteerism and philanthropy, has been an incubator for non-profits of all shapes and sizes. From the Rockefeller Foundation to the Gates Foundation, the U.S. has been home to some of the world's largest and most influential charitable organizations. The non-profit sector has contributed significantly to shaping public policy, advocating for social justice, and providing essential services to those in need.

In recent decades, the U.S. has seen a surge in the number of non-profits, indicating both an increased awareness of social issues and the growing activism of the populace. The sector has also grappled with challenges such as organizational sustainability, transparency, and the delicate balance between advocacy and political neutrality.

In the United States, the Internal Revenue Service (IRS) recognizes several classifications for non-profit organizations, each serving a unique purpose but unified in their aim to foster a better world. Here are the ten leading non-profit classifications recognized by the IRS today, alongside the criteria required to qualify for each:

501(c)(3) - Public Charities and Private Foundations

- **Purpose**: These organizations are established for religious, educational, charitable, scientific, or literary purposes. They can also qualify if they test for public safety, contribute to amateur sports competition, or prevent cruelty to children or animals.
- **Qualification Requirements**: Must operate exclusively for exempt purposes and none of its earnings may inure to the benefit of any private shareholder or individual.

501(c)(4) - Social Welfare Organizations

- **Purpose**: To promote social welfare by primarily focusing on the common good and general welfare of the community, such as by bringing about civic improvements and social advocacy.
- **Qualification Requirements**: Earnings must primarily benefit the general public, not private interests, and the promotion of social welfare does not include direct or indirect participation in political campaigns.

501(c)(5) - Labor, Agricultural, and Horticultural Organizations

- **Purpose**: To improve conditions of work, products, and efficiency in one's field of activity.
- **Qualification Requirements**: Activities must aim at the betterment of conditions of those

engaged in such pursuits, the improvement of grade or quality of their products, and the development of a higher degree of efficiency in their respective occupations.

501(c)(6) - Business Leagues, Chambers of Commerce

- **Purpose**: To promote the business interests of a community or improve business conditions of one or more lines of business.
- **Qualification Requirements**: It must not be organized for profit and no part of its net earnings may inure to the benefit of any private shareholder or individual.

501(c)(7) - Social and Recreational Clubs

- **Purpose**: To foster social or recreational activities for the benefit of its members.
- **Qualification Requirements**: The organization must be a club organized for pleasure, recreation, and other similar purposes and substantially all of its activities must be for such purposes.

501(c)(8) - Fraternal Beneficiary Societies and Associations

- **Purpose**: To provide for the payment of life, sickness, accident, or other benefits to members.
- **Qualification Requirements**: Must have a fraternal purpose, operate under the lodge system,

and provide for the payment of life, sickness, accident, or other benefits to the members.

501(c)(9) - Voluntary Employee Beneficiary Associations

- **Purpose**: To provide for payment of life, sickness, accident, or other benefits to members.
- **Qualification Requirements**: Membership must consist of employees who share some common employment-related bond, and the association must provide for the payment of benefits in accordance with members' rights set forth in its articles or bylaws.

501(c)(10) - Domestic Fraternal Societies and Associations

- **Purpose**: To carry out fraternal, cultural, religious, and social activities.
- **Qualification Requirements**: Must operate under the lodge system and devote its net earnings to charitable, fraternal, and cultural purposes.

501(c)(12) - Benevolent Life Insurance Associations, Mutual Ditch or Irrigation Companies, Mutual or Cooperative Telephone Companies, etc.

- **Purpose**: To provide a particular service (like insurance or communication) for the members or shareholders.

- **Qualification Requirements**: 85% or more of the income must come from members for the sole purpose of meeting losses and expenses.

501(c)(19) - Veterans' Organizations

- **Purpose**: To provide social and assistance services to veterans and their families.
- **Qualification Requirements**: The organization must be operated exclusively for charitable, educational, or recreational purposes that benefit the armed forces or those who have served in the armed forces, and at least 75% of members must be past or present members of the United States Armed Forces.

The vibrancy and diversity of the non-profit sector in the United States are clearly illuminated through these IRS classifications, showcasing a broad spectrum of causes and missions that these organizations champion. From the heartwarming support of public charities and private foundations to the community upliftment by social welfare organizations, and from the backbone of our workforce represented by labor and agricultural groups to the camaraderie and support within fraternal and veterans' organizations, the tapestry of non-profit work is rich and multifaceted.

Each classification not only serves a unique purpose in the ecosystem of philanthropy but also adheres to specific IRS requirements, ensuring their operations contribute positively to society while maintaining transparency and accountability. This array of classifications underscores the limitless potential for collective action and reaffirms the essential role non-profits play in fostering a more equitable, just, and vibrant world.

Whether through advancing education, championing social justice, or providing critical services, these organizations are the lifeblood of societal progress. The opportunity to engage with, support, or even establish a non-profit organization within these classifications is an open invitation to contribute to a legacy of change, progress, and hope that defines the very best of what it means to be part of a community dedicated to the greater good.

508 Compliance

Have you ever wondered about the intricate framework that supports non-profit organizations and the classifications that define their operations and guide their missions? Understanding the distinction between various types of non-profit organizations is not just about navigating legal jargon; it's about appreciating the heart of their commitment to serving public and communal needs.

Amidst the more commonly discussed 501(c) designations, there lies a less talked about but equally important classification – the 508 non-profit status. While the spotlight often shines brighter on its 501(c) counterparts, organizations under the 508 banner carry forward their missions with a quiet determination and an unwavering focus on service. But what makes the 508 classification stand out in the complex world of non-profits?

It's crucial to clarify that the IRS doesn't explicitly list "508 classifications" as it does with 501(c) ones. The essence of Section 508 of the Internal Revenue Code actually zeroes in on the requirements for non-profits to notify the Secretary of their tax-exempt status. Yet, the term "508 compliance" has gracefully entered the lexicon of non-profit organizations, especially among religious organizations and churches. These entities are automatically considered tax-exempt under Section 501(c)(3), yet they are not mandated to undergo the formal process of receiving recognition of their tax-exempt status from the IRS.

When we talk about "508 classifications," we're peeling back the layers to reveal the adherence of these organizations to crucial notification requirements. It's a testament to their faithfulness to governance and their commitment to transparency, ensuring they remain aligned with the legal frameworks designed to uphold their integrity and purpose.

Why, then, does this matter to us, standing at the crossroads of business, ministry, and philanthropy? Why should we care about the delineations of 508 compliance amidst the vast landscape of non-profit work?

Because understanding these classifications sheds light on the diversity and depth of the non-profit sector, inviting us to appreciate the varied ways in which organizations serve, inspire, and uplift communities around the globe.

The Modern Non-Profit Landscape

Gone are the days when non-profits were seen merely as adjuncts to the state or private sector. Today, they stand as stalwart partners in the democratic process, champions of justice and equality, crafting pathways of hope and resilience. Isn't it invigorating to witness such profound integration, to see non-profits at the forefront of shaping our collective destiny?

But what about the strategies that fuel their mission? Have you considered the innovative financial mechanisms that empower these organizations to weave their magic? Impact investing and social enterprise models are breaking new ground, blending commercial acumen with a laser focus on social missions. This fusion is not just about funding; it's about pioneering a new paradigm of sustainable change.

And then there's the digital revolution. Can you imagine

Non-Profit Creation

the power unlocked by democratizing access to technology? Non-profits are harnessing data and connectivity like never before, optimizing their impact, and reaching into the very heart of communities with precision and grace. It's a new dawn, one where technology becomes the catalyst for unprecedented levels of engagement and effectiveness.

Why does this matter, you might ponder? Why should we, standing at the confluence of faith, business, and ministry, immerse ourselves in understanding the modern non-profit landscape? Because it's here, amidst the hustle of innovation and the pulse of progress, that we find the essence of our calling.

In wrapping up our exploration of the "Legal Evolution of Non-Profits," it becomes clear that we stand at a pivotal moment in history. A moment where the legal frameworks surrounding non-profits are not just background mechanisms, but central pillars that support the dynamic and vital work of these organizations. The evolution we've witnessed, from the granular distinctions of 501(c) and 508 classifications to the modern non-profit landscape's integration of groundbreaking financial and technological strategies, underscores a profound transformation. This is not merely an era of change but an epoch of monumental progress in how non-profits operate and impact society.

The legal evolution of non-profits is a testament to our collective capability to adapt, innovate, and expand the boundaries of what's possible. It invites us, beckons us, to not only appreciate the complexity and diversity of the non-profit sector but to actively participate in its next chapter. Whether through advocacy, volunteering, or philanthropy, the call to action has never been clearer or more urgent. The fabric of our global society, woven through the hands of non-profits, relies on the continued vigilance, support, and engagement of us all.

As we pivot towards the future, let's carry forward the lessons learned and the insights gained with a spirit of enthusiasm, determination, and hope. The legal evolution of nonprofits is more than a narrative of change; it's a blueprint for building a better world. It's a journey we are all a part of, a call to arms in the most profound sense, urging us to lend our voices, our talents, our wisdom, our hands, and our hearts to the noble quest of nurturing a more just, equitable, and thriving global community.

Chapter 4

Setting up a Non-Profit

To the visionary souls who see beyond the horizon, who feel the stirring in their hearts to leverage their business savvy for a higher purpose, we extend our hands to you. Launching a non-profit organization is no mere administrative task; it is, indeed, a sacred mission. It's where faith breathes life into the mechanics of commerce, where every action is fueled by a deeper meaning.

Whether you are drawn to champion social justice, foster community growth, or address humanitarian needs, initiating your non-profit venture is much like embarking on a spiritual pilgrimage. In this chapter, we are not just helping you navigate through the complexities of bureaucracy, we are here to accompany you on a profound journey, transforming your divine calling into a tangible, impactful non-profit entity.

Every great non-profit organization begins not with concrete and contracts, but with a dream. It's in these dreams—visions of a better, kinder world—that the seeds of change are planted. But how does one bridge the gap between dreaming and doing? How does one turn a vision into reality?

The Prophetic Call to Action

When exactly do you feel that tug at your heartstrings? Is it in moments of quiet reflection, amid the day-to-day bustle, or through the gentle nudges that seem almost otherworldly in their origin? The genesis of every non-profit is rooted in a calling, a divine push towards championing a cause. It's crucial to pay attention to these moments. Like ancient prophets who meticulously recorded their visions, it's imperative to document these inklings. This act of recording transforms fleeting thoughts into a tangible plan, marking the sacred intersection where lofty ideals meet the groundwork of action.

Write your launch plan. The first step towards creating a meaningful non-profit is to envision it vividly. Think of your launch plan as a beacon that illuminates your organization's path, guiding you through both challenges and opportunities with unwavering clarity. It's essential to articulate this plan with compelling clarity—vague or uninspired language will not suffice to capture the full scope of your mission.

A truly impactful launch plan becomes part of your non-profit's foundation. It transcends the here and now, reaching into the future to inspire those who will carry on the legacy of your work. It should be audacious, unconfined by the present realities, acting as a vessel for your aspirations to soar. Imagine it as a bridge that connects your deepest hopes to the realm of possibility, inviting others to join in the continuous pursuit of a better world.

What does it mean to craft a launch plan that resonates beyond our time? How do we articulate a dream so powerful that it propels not just us, but future generations towards a shared goal? It's about daring to dream without bounds, to envisage a future that reflects our highest ideals and values.

This vision serves as more than just an organizational roadmap; it is the soul of your non-profit, breathing life into every strategy, decision, and action. It's the promise of what can be achieved when faith and purpose converge, inspiring a collective movement towards transformation and impact.

Write Your Purpose, Vision, Mission

The Purpose answers the question, "Why do we exist?" The Vision asks, "Where are we headed?", and the Mission provides an answer to "How do we get there?". It's crucial to craft these three elements in harmony as they collectively define the essence of your non-profit.

The Purpose
Why We Exist

At the core of every successful non-profit lies a compelling purpose—a reason for being that transcends individual gain and speaks to a higher calling. It's important to define this purpose with clarity, so it can serve as the foundation for all your future endeavors. What drives you towards creating this non-profit? How does it align with your values and beliefs? The Purpose is not just a statement—it's a guiding light that illuminates your journey.

The Vision
Where We're Headed

The Vision paints a vivid picture of the future your non-profit seeks to create complete with short and long term goals. This vision should not be limited by practical constraints or current realities; instead, it should be bold and ambitious, inspiring others to join in your cause. It's crucial to reflect on your purpose while crafting this vision as they are intrinsically connected. Your vision is the north star that guides your actions, keeping you on track towards creating lasting impact.

The Mission
How We'll Get There

The Mission statement provides a roadmap for achieving your vision. It outlines the specific goals and objectives that will lead to fulfilling your purpose. It answers the question, "How?" This statement should be actionable, measurable, and aligned with both your Purpose and Vision. A strong mission statement serves as a rallying cry, motivating your team and supporters towards a common goal.

The Power of Your Message

As you embark on this journey towards creating an impactful non-profit, never underestimate the power of your message. It's not just about the words you choose; it's about how those words are infused with passion and purpose. In a world inundated with information and distractions, it's crucial to craft a message that cuts through the noise and resonates deeply with your audience.

When sharing your non-profit's mission, don't be afraid to speak from the heart. Your passion for your cause will shine through in every word you say, compelling others to join you on this journey. Authenticity and vulnerability are powerful tools that can connect you with potential donors, volunteers, and supporters on a deeper level. By sharing your personal experiences and journey, you invite others to be part of something meaningful and transformative.

In a world where trends come and go, it's easy to get swept up in the latest fad or social media craze. However, it's crucial to stay true to your organization's core values and beliefs. These principles are the bedrock of your non-profit and should guide every decision you make, including your messaging. By staying authentic and consistent with your values, you build trust with your audience and establish a strong foundation for long-term impact.

Core Values

Just as a strong foundation is essential for a building to stand tall, core values are crucial for an organization's success. These guiding principles set the tone for your non-profit's culture and influence everything from decision-making to day-to-day operations. It's important to identify and define these values early on, ensuring they align with your Purpose, Vision, and Mission.

It's not enough to simply have a list of core values; they must be actively integrated into your organization's culture. This means modeling and reinforcing them through actions, policies, and communication. By living your values, you create a positive work culture that attracts like-minded individuals who are passionate about your cause.

In a world where shifting sands undermine fidelity, core values hold the firmament together. They are the heart of your non-profit, beating in sync with the community you serve. Without them, the noble edifice crumbles into a Dao-less endeavor.

Core values also serve as ethical guides, providing a moral compass for your organization. In an increasingly complex and interconnected world, it's crucial to have a set of values that guide decision-making and ensure integrity in all aspects of your non-profit's operations. By adhering to these values, you build trust with donors, partners, and the community at large.

What do you stand for? Honesty, integrity, empathy, courage—these aren't just words to adorn annual reports. When troubles assail, core values are the moral compass that guarantees fidelity to your mission. Choose them wisely, uphold them resolutely.

Officers

Every non-profit needs stewards—officers who are not just appointed personnel but anointed leaders. They must channel the sacred mantle of your organization and direct its energies with astute vision and servant hearts.

Your choice of officers is critical. Select individuals not just suited for the role but invested in the vision. Their commitment shouldn't be contractual but covenantal. They are the archangels of your operation, embodying the values they impart. They must be more than taskmasters; they should inspire, motivate, and uplift your team towards a common goal.

Choosing the President: The President is the leader of your non-profit, responsible for steering it towards fulfilling its purpose and achieving its vision. This role requires a unique blend of qualities: visionary thinking, strategic planning, effective communication, and strong leadership skills. When choosing a president, look for someone who embodies your core values and has a passion for your cause. They should also have experience in organizational management and a strong track record of achieving results.

The Vice President: The Vice President supports the President in their role and acts as a backup when needed. They should possess similar qualities to the President and be aligned with the organization's values, vision, and mission. It's also important for the Vice President to have complementary skills, bringing diversity of thought and perspective to the leadership team.

Secretary and Treasurer: The Secretary is responsible for maintaining records and ensuring compliance with legal requirements, while the Treasurer oversees the organization's finances. These roles require attention to detail, strong organizational skills, and a commitment to transparency and accountability. It's crucial to choose individuals with integrity and expertise in these areas to maintain the non-profit's credibility.

Board of Directors: The Board of Directors plays a crucial role in the governance of your non-profit. They provide oversight, strategic guidance, and support to the leadership team. It's essential to have a diverse board with a mix of skills, experience, and perspectives to provide well-rounded decision-making and ensure accountability.

Prayer Team: Last but certainly not least is the Prayer Team. If your non-profit has a spiritual aspect, it's vital to have a dedicated group of individuals who are committed to praying for the organization and its mission. These prayer warriors can provide essential support and guidance through their prayers and spiritual insights.

Articles of Incorporation

In the realm of non-profit organizations, the Articles of Incorporation stand as a foundational decree, much like a sacred scroll. This document is not merely administrative—it is the legal cornerstone that bestows your mission with a host of privileges, from tax exemptions to garnering the trust of your supporters. Think of it as the birth certificate for your organization, a testament to its legality and purpose in the world. When it comes time to draft this crucial document, seeking legal counsel is not just advisable; it's imperative. But this process is more than filling out forms; it's about encapsulating the essence of your mission. Your Articles should reflect the soul of your organization, outlining not only its structure but also its heart—a charitable purpose that elevates you beyond the realm of mere corporations, positioning your endeavor as a ministry cloaked in the guise of a non-profit.

Have you considered the power that lies within these Articles? How, by articulating your vision and mission with clarity and conviction, you're laying down a legal and spiritual foundation for your work?

Through drafting the Articles of Incorporation, you are not just complying with legal requirements; you are affirming your commitment to a cause greater than yourself. It's an opportunity to declare, in no uncertain terms, that your organization seeks to do more than just exist; it aims to make a difference, to serve, to uplift.

You should approach this task not as a mere formality but as a sacred act of dedication to your mission. In the careful crafting of your Articles, you have the power to set the tone for your organization's future, to build not just a legal entity but a beacon of hope and service.

Constitution and By-Laws

Within the foundational documents of your non-profit—the constitution and by-laws—resides the heart of your governance, the sacred commandments that guide your mission. These aren't mere formalities; they're the codified essence of your ministry's purpose and principles. But have you considered how these documents can serve not just your current needs but also the grand vision you have for the future?

The language we choose to enshrine in these documents must be both powerful and flexible. Why? Because as much as we plan, we must also allow room for the unexpected—for growth, for evolution. We urge you to write with not just the insight of today but with an eye towards a prosperous future. And yet, amidst this forward-looking optimism, a humble recognition of the profound responsibility we bear is essential. Governing a non-profit is no small task; it demands a commitment not only to the letter of the law but to the loftiest standards of integrity and faith.

How often do we pause to reflect on the significance of the words we commit to paper in our constitutions and by-laws? These documents are more than just guidelines; they are a declaration of our values, a blueprint for ethical leadership, and a covenant with the communities we serve.

Imagine the potential impact of our work when underpinned by documents that breathe life into our missions, that articulate our dreams with clarity and conviction, and that lay down the ethical and spiritual guardrails to guide us along our path.

Approach the crafting of your constitution and by-laws as a sacred act—a chance to lay a strong, flexible foundation for the incredible journey ahead. Consider this your opportunity to embed the very DNA of your mission into the bedrock of your organization, ensuring that every decision made and every action taken aligns with your core values and aspirations.

Elevator Speech

As a non-profit organization, one of the most effective tools you have in your arsenal is your elevator speech—a brief but impactful pitch that concisely explains your mission and why it matters. This powerful tool can be used in various settings, from networking events to meetings with potential donors and partners.

But what makes a successful elevator speech? It's not just about memorizing a script; it's about connecting with your audience and conveying the passion and purpose behind your organization.

When crafting your elevator speech, keep in mind that brevity is key. You want to grab your listener's attention and leave them wanting to know more. Start with a strong hook or headline that captures the essence of your mission, followed by a brief but impactful summary of what your organization does and why it matters.

Next, try to personalize your message by sharing a story or anecdote that illustrates the impact of your work. This will help your audience connect with your mission on an emotional level. Be sure to end with a clear call-to-action, whether it's asking for support or inviting the listener to learn more about your organization.

Remember, an elevator speech is not just about the words you say, but also how you say them. Be sure to speak with confidence and passion, making eye contact and using body language to convey your message. Practice your delivery in front of a mirror or with a friend to ensure that it comes across as authentic and impactful.

The foundational documents of your non-profit organization are not just legal requirements; they are powerful tools for aligning your mission with your governance, amplifying your impact, and inspiring others to join you in making a difference. So take the time and care to craft these documents with intention and purpose, imbuing them with the spirit of your organization's sacred mission. As you do, may your words and actions be guided by the highest standards of integrity and faith, and may your non-profit thrive as a beacon of hope and service in the world.

In the journey to establishing a non-profit, each step carries profound significance, from drafting your Articles of Incorporation to creating your Constitution and By-Laws and perfecting your Elevator Speech. These are not mere tasks to be checked off a list; they are the foundational pillars upon which your organization stands. Together, they form a sturdy framework that aligns your mission's spirit with its operational embodiment, ensuring governance and advocacy walk hand in hand towards achieving a shared vision.

Remember, the path of setting up a non-profit is both a legal and a spiritual voyage. It demands of you not just adherence to the rules of law but also a deep commitment to the values at the heart of your mission. It's about declaring to the world, with clarity and conviction, the difference you're poised to make. Through this process, you have the unique opportunity to craft an organization that is not only legally sound but ethically steadfast, one that inspires both the people it serves and those who join it in service.

By approaching each step with the weight it deserves, you ensure that your non-profit is built on a foundation of integrity, purpose, and unwavering dedication to your cause. May your efforts be fruitful, your vision clear, and your spirit undeterred. Here's to the beginning of a remarkable journey—the launching of a non-profit that will not merely exist but will thrive and foster change in the hearts of communities and individuals alike. The world awaits the positive impact your organization is destined to make.

Chapter 5

Raising Capital
For a Non-Profit Organization

Raising capital is a crucial aspect for any non-profit organization. Without proper funding, it can be challenging to execute programs and initiatives that are aimed at achieving the organization's mission. As a non-profit organization, your main goal is not to generate profits but rather to serve the community and achieve social impact. However, this does not mean that you should not focus on raising funds. In fact, having a steady stream of funding is essential for the sustainability and growth of your organization.

Funding the Vision

As a non-profit organization, securing funding is crucial for fulfilling your mission and making an impact. However, obtaining funding can be a daunting task, especially for new or small organizations.

But here's the thing - there are many sources of potential funding out there, and it's just a matter of finding the right fit for your organization. Whether it's through grants, donations, sponsorships, or partnerships, there are various avenues to explore. And with the right approach and strategy, you can successfully fund your vision.

The first step in securing funding is to do your research. Take the time to understand the different types of funding available and determine which ones align with your organization's mission and goals.

Grants are a popular option for non-profits, but they can also be highly competitive. Make sure to thoroughly research the eligibility requirements and application process before applying.

Individual donations are another significant source of funding, and building relationships with potential donors is key. Consider hosting fundraising events or creating a recurring giving program to engage donors in your cause.

Corporate sponsorships and partnerships are also worth exploring, as they can provide both funding and strategic support. Look for companies that align with your mission and values and approach them with a clear proposal outlining the benefits of collaboration.

When seeking funding, it's crucial to have a strong case for support. This includes a compelling narrative about your organization's impact, evidence of successful past projects, and a detailed budget and financial plan.

You should also be able to clearly articulate your organization's unique value proposition and how it sets you apart from others in the field. This will help potential funders see the relevance and potential impact of their support on your mission.

Once you have secured funding, it's essential to be a responsible steward of those resources. This means being transparent and accountable in your financial reporting, communicating regularly with your funders about the progress of their support, and expressing gratitude for their contributions.

By demonstrating responsible stewardship, you not only build trust with your current funders but also attract potential future donors who want to see their investments making a difference.

Finally, securing funding is crucial for fulfilling your mission and making a positive impact. By understanding the different types of funding available, building a strong case for support, and being responsible stewards of resources, you can successfully fund your vision and make a lasting difference in the world.

Keep persevering and advocating for your cause, and remember that every dollar raised brings you one step closer to achieving your mission.

The Art of Ministry Marketing

Marketing is often seen as a dirty word in the non-profit world, associated with commercialism and self-promotion. However, when done right, marketing can be a powerful tool for mission-driven organizations to reach new audiences and amplify their impact. A useful cliche' is,

"Find a need and fill it, See a tear and heal it."

Marketing for a ministry is unlike anything in the business world. It's about provoking thought, kindling emotion, and inspiring action. Every visual, every slogan, and every narrative thread must weave a tapestry of transformation.

Your ministry's story is your most potent marketing tool. Tell it without embellishment, but with the fervor that befits a gospel. Make it engaging, interactive, and shareable. Every soul touched by your narrative becomes a potential ally in your ministry.

By understanding the needs of your community and connecting with them in meaningful ways, you can effectively spread awareness about your organization and inspire others to support your cause.

Know Your Audience: The first step in effective marketing is to know your audience. Take the time to research and understand the demographics, interests, and behavior patterns of the people you are trying to reach. This will help you tailor your message and approach to resonate with them.

Once you know who you want to reach, it's essential to develop a compelling message that will capture their attention. This includes clearly stating your mission and the impact of your work in a concise and emotionally resonant way.

Your message should also be consistent across all your marketing channels, such as social media, website, and printed materials. This will help build brand recognition and trust among your audience.

Utilize Social Media: Social media has become a vital tool for organizations to connect with their supporters and spread their message. Choose the platforms that are most relevant to your target audience and regularly post engaging content that showcases the impact of your work.

It's also essential to engage with your followers by responding to comments, asking for feedback, and showing appreciation for their support. This will help build a sense of community around your organization and encourage others to get involved.

. . .

Leverage Visuals: In this digital age, visuals are crucial in capturing people's attention and conveying your message quickly. Utilize high-quality images and videos to showcase the impact of your work and create compelling stories that will inspire others to support your cause.

Collaborating with influencers is a new form of partnership. This means partnering with individuals or organizations who have a large following and align with your mission. Doing this helps expand your reach and credibility.

Therefore, You should seek out influencers in your community and work with them to promote your organization and spread awareness about your cause. Also remember, marketing is not just about promoting yourself; it's about creating meaningful connections with your audience and inspiring them to join you on your mission.

By understanding the needs of your community, crafting a compelling message, utilizing social media and visuals, and collaborating with influencers, you can effectively market your organization and make a greater impact in the world. So don't shy away from marketing, embrace it as a powerful tool to amplify your mission and create positive change.

Grant Funding Opportunities

Securing grant funding is a critical component of financial strategy for many non-profit organizations. It provides essential resources for project implementation, capacity building, and mission fulfillment. Understanding where to look for these opportunities can significantly increase your chances of success.

Government Grants: Government agencies at the local, state, and federal levels offer grants to non-profits for a variety of projects and programs. These grants often focus on specific areas such as health, education, social services, and environmental protection. Websites like Grants.gov in the United States serve as comprehensive resources, listing available grants and providing application guidelines.

Foundations: Numerous foundations around the world offer grants to non-profit organizations. These foundations, such as the Ford Foundation, the Rockefeller Foundation, and the Bill & Melinda Gates Foundation, focus on various causes, from global health and development to education and the arts. Each foundation has its criteria and application process, which can typically be found on their websites.

Corporate Giving Programs

Many corporations operate their own grant programs as part of their corporate social responsibility initiatives. Companies like Google, Microsoft, and Walmart offer grants to non-profits that align with their strategic goals, such as community development, sustainability, and education. Corporate grant programs often offer more than just financial support, including in-kind donations and volunteer time.

Non-Profit and Philanthropic Databases: Resources like the Foundation Center and Guidestar provide extensive databases of grant-giving organizations and foundations. These platforms offer tools to search for potential grants by focus area, geographic location, and funding amount, making it easier for non-profits to identify relevant funding opportunities.

Professional Associations: Depending on your organization's area of focus, professional associations related to your field may offer grants or have information on industry-specific funding sources. Membership in these associations often provides access to exclusive funding opportunities and valuable networking options.

Exploring these avenues for grant funding can open up numerous opportunities for your non-profit. It requires diligence, careful planning, and a strategic approach to identify and apply for the grants that best match your organization's needs and objectives. Remember, the key to successful grant funding is not just to find the right opportunities but to also submit well-researched, compelling applications that stand out to funders.

Potential Grant Funding Companies for Non-Profit Ministries

1. **The Lilly Endowment Inc.** - Specializes in the support of religious, educational, and community development initiatives, making it an ideal candidate for non-profit ministries.
2. **The Arthur Vining Davis Foundations** - Provides grants to religious institutions for projects that enrich spiritual practices and foster interfaith understanding.
3. **The Henry Luce Foundation** - Offers funding through its Religion and Theology program, supporting projects that enhance the understanding of religion and promote inter-religious dialogue.

4. **The John Templeton Foundation** - Funds initiatives at the intersection of science and religion, encouraging dialogue and exploring how religious beliefs can interact with the scientific understanding of the universe.
5. **The Conrad N. Hilton Foundation** - Awards grants to Catholic sisters and their ministries, focusing on efforts that alleviate human suffering and promote global well-being.
6. **The E. Rhodes and Leona B. Carpenter Foundation** - Supports religious, educational, and cultural programs, including those offered by non-profit ministries.
7. **The M.J. Murdock Charitable Trust** - Primarily serves the Pacific Northwest with grants for projects that enrich life in the region, including religious and spiritual development.
8. **The DeMoss Foundation** - Provides support to Christian organizations and projects that align with its mission of spreading the Christian gospel and serving the needy.
9. **The Mustard Seed Foundation** - Offers grants to churches and ministries around the world, focusing on initiatives that promote the Christian faith.
10. **The Kern Family Foundation** - Supports educational and religious initiatives that foster a good, industrious, and prosperous society, with specific programs aimed at integrating faith, work, and economics.

The following is contact information for five of the aforementioned Grant Funding Companies.

Non-Profit Creation

The Lilly Endowment Inc.

Website: https://www.lillyendowment.org/

- **Contact Email:** info@lillyendowment.org
- **Phone Number:** (317) 924-5471
- **Address:** 2801 North Meridian Street, Indianapolis, Indiana 46208, USA

The Templeton Foundation

Website: https://www.templeton.org/

- **Contact Email:** inquiries@templeton.org
- **Phone Number:** (215) 887-8333
- **Address:** 300 Conshohocken State Road, Suite 500, West Conshohocken, Pennsylvania 19428, USA

The Mustard Seed Foundation

Website: http://www.msfdn.org/

- **Contact Email:** contact@msfdn.org
- **Phone Number:** (703) 524-5620
- **Address:** 7115 Leesburg Pike, #304, Falls Church, Virginia 22043, USA

The M.J. Murdock Charitable Trust

Website: https://murdocktrust.org/

- **Contact Email:** info@murdocktrust.org

Jonathan & Donna Vorce

- **Phone Number:** (360) 694-8415
- **Address:** 655 West Columbia Way, Suite 700, Vancouver, Washington 98660, USA

The Arthur Vining Davis Foundations

Website: https://www.avdf.org/

- **Contact Email:** info@avdf.org
- **Phone Number:** (904) 359-0670
- **Address:** 1300 Riverplace Blvd, Suite 700, Jacksonville, Florida 32207, USA

By reaching out to these organizations through their provided contact information, non-profit ministries can explore potential grant funding opportunities that align with their mission and objectives.

Exploring funding opportunities with these organizations can provide vital resources for non-profit ministries to fulfill their mission and expand their impact. Each foundation has its distinctive focus and application process, so ministries should thoroughly research and align their proposals to meet the specific criteria and objectives of the funder. With dedication and strategic planning, non-profit ministries can secure the necessary funding to carry out their vital work in the community.

Overall, understanding the various sources of grant funding and tailoring your approach to meet each funder's requirements is crucial for successful grant acquisition. By continuously seeking out new opportunities, building relationships with funders, and submitting well-crafted proposals, non-profits can increase their chances of securing essential funding to support their programs and initiatives.

Remember, grants not only provide financial resources but also validation and recognition for the impactful work that non-profits do in our communities. So keep exploring, stay persistent, and never give up on your organization's mission!

Legacy Giving to Non-Profit Ministries

Legacy giving, also known as planned giving, allows benefactors to leave a lasting impact on non-profit ministries they care about. Here are several ways to be involved:

1. **Bequests in a Will or Trust:** One of the simplest ways to contribute. A benefactor can designate a specific dollar amount, a percentage of their estate, or a particular asset to a non-profit ministry in their will or trust.
2. **Beneficiary Designations:** Many financial accounts, including retirement accounts, life insurance policies, and bank or brokerage accounts, allow the owner to name a beneficiary upon their death. Naming a non-profit ministry as a partial or full beneficiary is a straightforward way to support the ministry's future work.
3. **Charitable Gift Annuities:** This method involves a benefactor making a gift to a non-profit ministry in exchange for a fixed, annual income for life. It's a way to donate while also securing income during retirement years.
4. **Charitable Remainder Trusts:** These trusts enable a benefactor to receive income (or provide income to another individual) for a lifetime or a term of years after which the remaining trust assets are transferred to the non-profit ministry.

5. **Charitable Lead Trusts:** Inverse to a charitable remainder trust, a charitable lead trust provides income to the non-profit ministry for a number of years, after which the remaining trust assets go back to the benefactor or their heirs.
6. **Real Estate Gifts:** Benefactors can gift real estate to a non-profit ministry either during their lifetime or through their estate. This can include homes, land, and other types of real property.
7. **Endowments:** Contributing to or establishing an endowed fund can provide a non-profit ministry with a sustainable source of income, where the principal gift remains intact in perpetuity, and only the investment income is used.

By engaging in legacy giving, benefactors ensure their generosity benefits future generations and supports the continued success of non-profit ministries. Each option has specific tax implications and benefits, so it's advisable for donors to consult with financial and legal advisors to determine the best way to support their favored ministries and make a lasting impact.

Foundations and Non-Profit Funding

The synergy between foundations and non-profit organizations plays a pivotal role in enabling social, educational, and environmental advancements. Foundations, whether family-owned, corporate, or independent, are instrumental in providing the financial backbone for many non-profit initiatives. This financial aid comes in various forms, including grants, scholarships, and project funding, designed to support non-profits in achieving their goals.

Non-Profit Creation

Foundations typically have specific areas of interest or causes they support, ranging from healthcare and education to environmental conservation and social justice. Non-profits seeking funding must align their projects or missions with the foundation's objectives to increase their chances of receiving support. The application process for funding can be competitive and rigorous, requiring detailed proposals, clear objectives, and evidence of potential impacts.

The relationship is mutually beneficial. While non-profits benefit from the financial resources and credibility associated with foundation grants, foundations fulfill their mission of contributing to societal improvement through supporting effective and impactful projects. Furthermore, this collaboration often extends beyond financial support, involving capacity building, strategic advice, and networking opportunities that can be crucial for a non-profit's growth and sustainability.

For non-profit organizations, understanding the landscape of foundation funding, staying informed about application cycles, and building relationships with potential funders are vital steps towards securing the necessary resources to carry out their mission. Successful partnerships with foundations not only provide financial support but also leverage resources, knowledge, and networks that can amplify a non-profit's impact on the community it serves.

In conclusion, raising capital for a non-profit corporation is a multifaceted endeavor that requires a deep understanding of the funding landscape and a strategic approach to engaging potential donors and grant-making organizations. The opportunities for financial support are varied and often specific to the organization's mission, objectives, and geographical location. Non-profit leaders must be adept at navigating this complex environment, leveraging their networks, and effectively communicating the value and impact of their work to secure the necessary funds.

The foundations and trusts listed in this chapter represent just a fraction of the potential sources of support available to non-profits. By crafting compelling proposals, building strong relationships with funders, and maintaining a commitment to their mission, non-profit corporations can access the capital needed to further their invaluable contributions to society.

Remember, the pursuit of funding is not just about financial gain; it is an opportunity to tell your story, broaden your impact, and forge meaningful partnerships that can endure well into the future.

Chapter 6

Non-Profit Finances

If there's one thing that will trip a ministry up its finances. When you're dealing with money, things can get tricky quickly. But in order to keep a ministry running and provide necessary services to the community, managing finances is crucial. It requires a sharp blend of intelligence and awareness. Whether it's gracefully accepting donations from generous supporters or judiciously planning expenses, every decision must be guided by a strategic financial plan. This chapter helps guide you in utilizing the resources available to you efficiently without compromising the organization's ethical values or leaving donors with the impression of being exploited.

For non-profits determined to lead their cause, understanding the nuances of financial responsibility isn't optional; it's essential. This exploration of non-profit finances serves as an inspiring guide for organizations aiming to grasp the complexities of their financial situation and to forge a viable path towards achieving their mission.

In the distinctive realm of non-profits, where each dollar symbolizes the labor of the working class and embodies a promise of hope, developing financial acumen is a reflection of the organization's ability to transform noble intentions into significant impact.

By mastering financial management, non-profits can indeed live out their calling, empowering communities, and making a tangible difference. Remember, in the pursuit of your mission, financial literacy isn't just beneficial; it's transformative.

The Ethical Compass of Non-Profit Salaries

The compass needle of financial stewardship shouldn't shy away from discussing salaries within a non-profit structure. Salaries must be both competitive enough to draw qualified individuals and conservative enough to maintain the fiscal integrity of the organization. Here's how:

Appropriate Compensation
for Non-Profit Directors

Directors play a pivotal role in shaping the direction and success of an organization, holding significant sway over its strategic path. Given this influential position, it is crucial that their compensation reflects a careful balance between their extensive experience, the weight of their responsibilities, and the need for economic prudence. While high salaries are deemed equitable and often necessary in the competitive landscape of the for-profit sector, they can inadvertently cast a shadow on the altruistic mission and perception of non-profit organizations. Therefore, maintaining transparency throughout the process of determining director pay becomes paramount to uphold the integrity and trust in these organizations.

A widely praised method to ensure fairness and accountability in setting director salaries is the utilization of comprehensive market salary data. This approach involves a thorough analysis of compensation levels across similar positions in the industry, taking into account factors such as organization size, budget, and geographic location. By benchmarking against this data, organizations can ascertain appropriate compensation levels that are competitive yet mindful of their budgetary constraints and mission-driven goals. This not only aids in attracting and retaining talented leaders but also reassures donors of the organization's commitment to fiscal responsibility and ethical practices.

The Matter of the Secretary

Administrative roles, though they may not always stand in the spotlight like board positions do, are absolutely essential "the sine qua non" for ensuring operational efficiency within any organization. These positions, especially that of a secretary, involve a wide range of responsibilities that are critical for the smooth running of daily operations. A secretary's compensation should, therefore, be carefully calibrated to reflect their level of experience, the breadth and depth of their administrative responsibilities, and the cost of living in their locality. This is because the work they do is like an invisible thread that meticulously stitches together the various aspects of the organization, holding it together in a coherent, functional unit. Their role in maintaining the fabric of the organization cannot be overstated, and as such, deserves a level of remuneration that is thoughtfully reflective of their invaluable contribution.

Mileage and Travel Allowances

Non-profit organizations are fundamentally built on the principles of community and connectivity, key elements that often require their staff to engage in considerable amounts of travel to foster these vital connections. This travel, essential for meeting with stakeholders, partners, and communities, means that mileage and travel allowances, often encapsulated into per diem rates, become more than just fiscal provisions. They are, in fact, tangible acknowledgments of the personnel's unwavering dedication and hard work in advancing the organization's mission. Such allowances should be thoughtfully designed to serve as a comprehensive support platform. This ensures that those passionate individuals committed to the cause can travel without worrying about financial burdens, yet also prevents any possibility of excessive spending. By doing so, it balances the need for operational efficiency with the genuine appreciation of the staff's efforts, making sure that the organization's resources are used effectively while also valuing its most important asset: its people.

The Suggested Overall Percentage

Quantifying the exact percentage of an organization's budget that should be allocated to personnel costs is an intricate exercise in maintaining subtlety and precision. Striking the perfect balance between meeting operational needs and fostering strategic growth often showcases the judicious and thoughtful application of available funds. It's a delicate decision-making process that financial managers face, where common practice suggests that personnel costs should typically range between 25-35% of the total budget. However, this is not a one-size-fits-all rule. Flexibility within these bounds is crucial, as it reveals a financial policy that is responsive and alive to the organization's evolving needs and circumstances.

This flexibility allows for an organization, such as ministries, to adapt its financial strategies in response to changing operational demands or strategic opportunities. Staying within the recommended percentage range enables ministries to strike a harmonious balance, investing adequately in their workforce while also ensuring sufficient funds are directed towards programs and services that further their mission. This is particularly important in sectors where human capital is paramount to the success and impact of the organization's work.

The delicate balance between personnel costs and other expenditures necessitates meticulous financial planning and oversight. It requires a deep understanding of the organization's mission, strategic objectives, and the external environment in which it operates. Effective and ethical management of the ministry's resources involves not just meeting current needs but also anticipating future challenges and opportunities. By carefully navigating these considerations, organizations can optimize their resource allocation, ensuring they are both supporting their workforce and advancing their mission in a sustainable and impactful manner.

Administrative Costs

Administrative costs, though not always visible, play a crucial role in the background, acting as essential pillars of support for the smooth day-to-day operation of non-profit organizations. These costs cover a wide range of expenses, from employee salaries and office supplies to technology systems that keep the organization running efficiently. Demystifying these costs by breaking them down and understanding their importance ensures that they receive the attention and funding they deserve, without becoming a financial burden that detracts from the organization's mission. By doing so, non-profits can allocate resources more effectively, ensuring their sustainability and continued ability to serve their communities.

Compensation for
Office Personnel and Workers

In the world of non-profit organizations, the human element is absolutely non-negotiable. Competent office personnel and dedicated workers serve as the custodians of order and efficiency, ensuring that operations run smoothly and effectively. These individuals play a crucial role in the day-to-day successes of non-profits, warranting a pay scale that adequately respects and acknowledges their invaluable contribution.

Differentiating salaries across various skill levels and responsibilities is not just a matter of fairness; it's a strategic approach to simplifying the compensation charticle. By doing so, organizations can ensure that salaries accurately reflect the level of service and commitment each employee brings to the table, across all levels of the administrative board. This approach not only promotes transparency in how compensation is determined but also reinforces the organization's commitment to equity and fairness, thereby enhancing job satisfaction and motivation among staff.

Supplies and Services

From the ink that signs the physical checks to the tactile computer keyboards used to draft electronic ones, the myriad of supplies and services quietly underpin the organizational flow, often unnoticed. These essential tools, when procured both ethically and economically, are the unsung heroes that enable non-profits to operate efficiently. By carefully selecting these provisions, non-profits can ensure that a larger portion of their resources is directed towards the actualization of their mission, thereby maximizing their impact on the community and beyond. This strategic approach to resource allocation not only enhances operational efficiency but also reinforces the organization's commitment to ethical practices and stewardship.

Navigating Advertising Costs

In a world overflowing with countless narratives, the necessity for effective advertising cannot be overstated; it's a definitive requirement, not merely an option. Storytelling, especially for non-profits, transcends being just a mere necessity; it elevates into an art form that demands mastery and finesse. The financial implications of deploying this art form in communication strategies should ideally align with the broader financial strategy of the organization. It's paramount that every dollar invested in advertising is accounted for, ensuring a clear and measurable path to return on investment. This return could manifest in various forms - enhanced brand visibility, a wider reach in volunteer recruitment efforts, or a significant increase in donor acquisition. Each aspect of the investment in advertising should be meticulously planned to contribute towards achieving the organization's overarching goals.

Event Planning

Non-profit events stand as a critical pivot point for community engagement, serving not only as gatherings but also as a reflection of the organization's mission and values. The choreography of these events, therefore, demands meticulous planning and financial prudence to ensure they resonate with their intended audience. The cost calculation for these events, far from being an arbitrary task, should be a carefully considered process. Instead of being a divergent art, it should align meticulously with the event's intended outcome. This involves paying homage to fiscal responsibility, ensuring that every dollar spent contributes towards creating an experience that not only meets the logistical needs of the event but also deeply resonates with the non-profit's ethos. It is about striking the perfect balance between creating an impactful and memorable event, and maintaining the financial health of the organization, ensuring that the event serves as a true extension of the non-profit's core values and mission.

The Three Pillars of Fiscal Responsibility

Money is NOT the root of all evil!

"The LOVE of money is the root of all evil."
~ 1 Timothy 6:10.

In fact, the Bible clearly states,

"Money answereth all things."
~ Ecclesiastes 10:19

Money, alongside its origins and management methods, represents a formidable trilogy in the realm of non-profit organizations.

1. This epic narrative begins with the ethical sourcing of funds, a critical process that involves not only identifying potential donors but also ensuring that

the funds are raised in a manner that aligns with the organization's values and missions.
2. Following this, the storyline seamlessly transitions into the complex and almost magical alchemy of resource allocation. Here, the emphasis is on the strategic distribution of these funds across various projects and initiatives, maximizing impact while maintaining financial sustainability.
3. The final act of this trilogy merges into a celestial choreography of meticulous record-keeping and transparent reporting. This stage is crucial for maintaining accountability to donors, stakeholders, and regulatory bodies, ensuring that every penny is accounted for and its use is clearly communicated.

Together, these three pillars uphold the financial integrity and operational efficacy of non-profit entities, allowing them to thrive and make a lasting impact in their respective domains.

The pursuit of funds by a non-profit organization should reflect the essential principles and values that are at the heart of its mission. This means maintaining a high level of transparency in all interactions with donors, clearly and unambiguously articulating how their contributions will be utilized, and demonstrating an unwavering commitment to the cause they support. These three priorities

- transparency,
- clear communication, and
- commitment

are what non-profits should prioritize when seeking financial support.

Ethical fundraising practices are not only crucial for maintaining and enhancing an organization's reputation; they also play a significant role in building and sustaining a donor base that is deeply rooted in trust and mutual respect. By adhering to these ethical guidelines, non-profits can ensure that their fundraising efforts are successful in the long term, thereby securing the resources they need to continue making a positive impact on the communities they serve.

Allocating Money in the Non-Profit

Financial allocation within organizations, particularly non-profits, transcends the mere act of distributing funds; it embodies a methodology centered on maximizing impact. Each financial decision undergoes rigorous scrutiny to ensure alignment with the organization's overarching mission. Executive meetings dedicated to financial allocation emphasize the significance of programmatic spending. This approach advocates for a strategic dispersion of funds across projects, aiming to achieve an equitable distribution that enhances community benefits.

Key Principles of Effective Financial Allocation

- **Strategic Planning:** Financial resources are allocated following a strategic plan that aligns with the organization's goals. This ensures that every expenditure contributes directly to the mission's advancement.

- **Evidence-based Decision Making:** Decisions on fund allocation are supported by data and evidence, reinforcing the importance of investing in areas that yield the highest impact on the community.

- **Equitable Distribution:** A fair distribution of resources across various projects is essential. This strategy ensures that all initiatives receive adequate funding to achieve their objectives, maximizing the overall benefit to the community.

- **Continuous Evaluation:** The process involves regular assessments to measure the effectiveness of financial allocations. Adjustments are made based on these evaluations to optimize the impact of future spending.

The Importance of Programmatic Spending

Programmatic spending refers to the allocation of funds directly towards programs and initiatives that further the organization's mission. This contrasts with administrative or overhead costs, focusing investment on activities with direct community impact. The rationale behind programmatic spending is to ensure that the majority of resources are utilized in service delivery, enhancing the organization's ability to achieve its objectives and provide tangible benefits to the community.

By adopting a science-driven approach to financial allocation, organizations can enhance their capacity to make informed decisions, prioritize investments in high-impact areas, and demonstrate a commitment to achieving measurable outcomes. This methodology not only optimizes resource utilization but also fosters transparency and accountability, building trust among stakeholders.

Effective financial allocation is a critical component of organizational management, requiring a meticulous and strategic approach to ensure that every investment contributes meaningfully to the mission. By focusing on programmatic spending, organizations can maximize their impact, delivering substantial benefits to the communities they serve.

Maintaining Records and Receipts

"There is protection in covering and accountability."

In the realm of financial management, meticulous record-keeping and the preservation of receipts play a pivotal role far beyond mere regulatory compliance. These documents act as the cornerstones of financial accountability, providing a transparent and verifiable trail of all monetary transactions within an organization. This practice encompasses the entire spectrum of financial activities, ranging from everyday expenditures, such as purchasing coffee, to significant financial inflows like grants.

The primary function of keeping comprehensive records and receipts is to furnish tangible evidence of the organization's financial activities. This evidence-based approach ensures that every dollar spent or received is accounted for, thereby underpinning the principles of fiscal responsibility:

1. **Transparency:** Detailed records offer clear insight into the financial workings of an organization, promoting transparency with stakeholders.
2. **Accuracy:** Proper documentation aids in maintaining accurate financial statements, crucial for internal assessments and external reporting.
3. **Compliance:** Adherence to regulatory requirements is facilitated by exhaustive record-

keeping, mitigating risks associated with audits and legal scrutiny.
4. **Strategic Decision-Making:** Analyzing historical financial data enables informed decision-making, guiding strategic planning and resource allocation.
5. **Fiscal Stewardship:** Demonstrating prudent management of financial resources reaffirms the organization's commitment to its mission and values.

Techniques for Effective Record-Keeping

To ensure the efficacy of this foundational practice, organizations may employ several techniques:

- **Digital Archiving:** Leveraging technology to digitize and securely store financial documents enhances accessibility and reduces the risk of loss or damage.
- **Regular Audits:** Conducting periodic reviews of financial records ensures ongoing accuracy and compliance with established standards.
- **Training Programs:** Educating staff on the significance and methodologies of effective record-keeping can foster a culture of accountability and diligence.

Incorporating visual aids such as charts and graphs can significantly augment the comprehensibility of financial records, offering at-a-glance insights into spending patterns, budget allocations, and financial health. Meanwhile, illustrative narratives contextualizing financial transactions can enhance engagement, providing stakeholders with relatable scenarios that underscore the importance of each documented expenditure.

Therefore, the diligent maintenance of records and receipts transcends its basic function as a compliance measure. It embodies the rigorous safeguarding of financial integrity, serving as a testament to the organization's dedication to responsible stewardship of its resources. Through structured and evidence-based practices, organizations can not only fulfill their fiduciary duties but also bolster stakeholder confidence in their operational efficacy and ethical governance.

Integrity and Transparency in Non-Profit Finances

In the realm of non-profit finance, the concepts of integrity and transparency are not simply fashionable terms; they symbolize the foundational pillars of budgetary responsibility. These principles serve to uphold the ethical standards that are crucial for the successful operation and public trust in non-profit organizations.

The Role of Annual Reports
in Financial Transparency

The production of an annual report, which provides a detailed account of a non-profit's financial activities over the year, transcends a mere requirement by tax regulators such as the IRS. This document offers a vital platform for engaging with stakeholders, including donors, volunteers, and the communities served. It presents an opportunity to demonstrate the organization's commitment to financial prudence and to narratively illustrate how fiscal decisions align with its mission and values.

Effective annual reports go beyond listing figures; they weave the financial data into a coherent story that highlights achievements, challenges overcome, and the impact of the organization's work. By doing so, they offer transparency and foster a deeper connection with the audience, reinforcing trust and support.

The Imperative of Sharing
Financial Health

Non-profits operate within a broader ecosystem that thrives on mutual respect and trust among all participants, including donors, beneficiaries, and the wider community. Openness regarding financial health is not optional but a duty that non-profits owe to this ecosystem. Communicating about financial matters, whether it involves successes or challenges, is crucial in maintaining an environment of transparency.

This process involves more than just sharing numbers; it requires providing context, explaining financial decisions, and discussing their impact. Such openness nurtures an environment where stakeholders feel informed and involved, thereby strengthening the foundation of mutual trust. This shared understanding reassures all parties of the non-profit's commitment to not only being fiscally responsible but also transparent and open in its financial dealings.

To achieve this level of transparency, non-profits can employ various strategies, including regular financial updates through newsletters, detailed breakdowns of expenditures in relation to project outcomes, and forums for questions and discussions about financial strategies. These approaches ensure that the financial narrative of the non-profit is accessible and understandable to all, thereby reinforcing the values of integrity and transparency.

Integrity and transparency are not merely aspirational goals but practical necessities in the governance of non-profit organizations. Through clear communication, structured reporting, and open dialogue about financial health, non-profits can foster an environment of trust and accountability. These efforts not only fulfill ethical obligations but also strengthen the bonds with the community, ensuring sustained support and success in fulfilling their missions.

In closing, the stewardship of non-profit finances necessitates a steadfast commitment to integrity, transparency, and meticulous management. The implementation of effective record-keeping practices, the production of insightful annual reports, and the proactive sharing of financial health are paramount in upholding these values. These actions not only satisfy regulatory requirements and foster trust among stakeholders but also reinforce the non-profit's dedication to its mission and ethical governance. Through adherence to these principles, non-profit organizations can ensure their financial practices reflect their core values and contribute to their long-term success and sustainability. Thus, the careful management of finances is not merely a procedural necessity but a reflection of the organization's integrity and commitment to making a positive impact in the community it serves.

Chapter 7

Mastering the Art of Non-Profit Board Meetings

Non-profit organizations play a crucial role in our society, addressing important social issues and providing support to those in need. These organizations rely heavily on the guidance and leadership of their board of directors. Board meetings are an essential part of running a non-profit organization, as they provide a platform for decision-making, strategic planning, and accountability.

As a board member or potential board member, it is important to understand the intricacies of non-profit board meetings and master the art of making them effective and efficient. Here are some tips to help you become a valuable asset to your non-profit organization's board:

- **Come prepared:** Board meetings often involve discussions on complex issues and strategic planning. It is crucial that every board member comes prepared with relevant materials, such as reports, financial statements, and meeting agendas. This will not only save time during the meeting but also show your commitment to the organization's mission and goals.

- **Actively participate:** Board meetings are not just for listening, but also for actively participating in discussions and decision-making processes. Don't be afraid to share your ideas and opinions, as they may contribute to finding innovative solutions and strategies for the organization. However, be mindful of other board members' viewpoints and work towards reaching a consensus.

- **Stay focused and respectful:** Keeping discussions on track and maintaining a respectful tone is essential for productive board meetings. Avoid getting sidetracked by personal agendas or conflicts, and always show respect towards your fellow board members. Remember that all decisions should be made in the best interest of the organization, not individual interests.

- **Be accountable:** As a board member, you have a responsibility to ensure the non-profit organization is fulfilling its mission and goals effectively. This includes staying informed about the organization's progress, asking questions, and holding yourself and others accountable for their actions. By being proactive in your role as a board member, you can help drive positive change and ensure the organization's success.

- **Continuously improve:** Non-profit organizations are constantly evolving, and so should their board meetings. As a board member, it is important to continuously evaluate the effectiveness of board meetings and suggest improvements. This can include implementing new technologies for virtual meetings, creating committees for specific tasks, or adjusting meeting structures to better suit the organization's needs.

By mastering the art of non-profit board meetings, you can make a significant impact on your organization and its mission. Your dedication and active involvement will not only benefit the organization but also contribute to creating positive change in our society. So, embrace your role as a board member and continuously strive to improve board meetings for the betterment of your non-profit organization.

The Chairman of the Board

At the helm of every non-profit board meeting stands the Chairman — a key figure responsible for steering the meeting in the right direction. This individual isn't just tasked with leading discussions but with creating an environment where all participants feel empowered to share their insights. Here's what a chairman should embody:

1. **Clarity and Focus**: The Chairman should bring clarity to complex topics, ensuring members understand the agenda and what is expected of them.
2. **Diplomacy and Inclusivity**: Every board is a microcosm of the community it serves, and the Chairman must ensure a diversity of voices is not only heard but also respected and included.

3. **Strategic Leadership**: The Chairman must be able to see the big picture, keeping the board focused on long-term strategies rather than getting bogged down by minutiae.
4. **Meeting Management**: Balancing participation, timing, and adherence to the agenda is a critical facet of the Chairman's role. Effective time management keeps meetings from derailing.

In addition, the Chairman needs to be well-versed on the organization's by-laws, policies, and procedures, and be adept in utilizing parliamentary procedure to govern group discussions.

Robert's Rules of Order

In the realm of non-profit organizations, the beacon that has illuminated the path for effective meeting management and decision-making processes for generations is none other than Robert's Rules of Order.* Have you ever pondered upon the importance of having a structured set of guidelines to bring order, fairness, and dignity to your meetings? What about the power of having every voice heard, ensuring that both the majority and minority opinions are given equal respect and consideration?

- **Order and Decorum Prevail:** Imagine stepping into a meeting where chaos and confusion reign supreme. Now, contrast that with a gathering where every discussion, debate, and decision

---

* Henry M. Robert III, Daniel H. Honemann, Thomas J. Balch, et al., *Robert's Rules of Order Newly Revised* (11th edition, Da Capo Press, 2011).

transpires in an orderly, democratic, and dignified manner. This is the essence of what Robert's Rules of Order brings to the table - an environment steeped in uniformity and respect, where decisions are not just made, but made right.

- **All Voices Can Be Heard:** In the heart of every thriving organization lies the principle of inclusivity, where each member's voice is valued, and every opinion matters. But how do we ensure that this principle is upheld? By adopting Robert's Rules of Order, we safeguard the rights of both the majority and the minority, making sure that the floor is open for all to express themselves.

- **Business Can Be Concluded:** At first glance, the intricacies of Robert's Rules might appear daunting. Yet, their true purpose is to streamline processes, making it possible for business to be concluded swiftly and effectively. Imagine having a framework that ensures every member gets a chance to speak, and decisions are reached through a majority vote, efficiently and fairly.

By weaving Robert's Rules into the very fabric of your non-profit board meetings, you're not just adopting a set of procedures; you're fostering a culture of productive governance, rooted in a tradition of fairness and equity.

This is more than just about following rules; it's about living out the calling of your organization with integrity, unity, and a profound respect for the democratic process.

Organizing The Agenda

In the heart of every board meeting lies the agenda, a sacred map guiding the path of discussion and decision-making. Have you ever pondered how a meticulously crafted agenda can transform your meeting into a vessel for not just business, but ministry? How can it set the stage for an assembly that not only meets the eye but touches the soul?

Pre-Meeting Preparation - The Foundation of Success: Before the meeting even begins, the Chairman, alongside the Executive Director, engages in a dance of diligence and discernment. Together, they sculpt the agenda to reflect the organization's heartbeat - its current needs, aspirations, and divine calling. This sacred preparatory act is not merely about staying informed; it's about staying aligned with the organization's mission and the higher purpose it serves.

Item Prioritization - The Art of Divine Focus: In the realm of board governance, not all topics hold equal weight. Some, like strategic plans and financial stewardship, demand our utmost attention and time. They are the pillars upon which our organization stands, requiring significant deliberation and divine wisdom. How do we discern what matters most? By prioritizing agenda items with a spirit-led heart, ensuring that the urgent does not overshadow the important, we honor our commitment to both our mission and our Maker.

Time Management - A Testament to Wisdom: Assigning estimated times to each agenda item is a practice of wisdom, a testimony to our respect for the value of each moment bestowed upon us. This discipline enables us to dwell not just on the pressing, but also on the profound, ensuring that meaningful discussions are not sacrificed on the altar of efficiency.

Inclusion of All Necessary Items - The Commitment to Integrity: The agenda, in its completeness, must stand as a beacon of compliance, transparency, and integrity. Including standard items such as approval of minutes, committee reports, and new business is not just a nod to non-profit regulations; it's a testament to our commitment to accountability before both man and God. Does this not reflect our dedication to governance that is not only effective but righteous?

By crafting an agenda that mirrors the sanctity of our mission, we chart a course for meetings that transcend the mundane, embodying the essence of ministry and business intertwined. This is not just about running meetings; it's about fostering gatherings that are imbued with purpose, passion, and the presence of the Holy Spirit.

Unlock the potential of your organization by elevating your board meetings from mere administrative tasks to acts of worship and stewardship. Live out your calling with fervor, and witness how your organization can indeed be a light unto the world.

Keeping Minutes

Have you ever considered the power held within the pages of your non-profit's board meeting minutes?* These documents are not merely a bland recounting of events; they are the very fabric of history being woven in real-time. Imagine, for a moment, the legacy left behind through these pages – a testament to the decisions, the visions, and the divine guidance steering the organization forward. How then, do we ensure these minutes truly capture the essence of our meetings?

- **Reflect the True Proceedings:** The core of accurate minutes lies in their ability to mirror the heart and soul of the meeting. Every question posed, every motion made, and every answer given, especially when it pertains to pivotal decisions like financial strategies or policy shifts, must be recorded with precision. Aren't these the moments that shape the future of our mission, crafting a roadmap for those who will follow in our footsteps?

- **Highlight Responsible Parties:** With each decision penned down, there arises a call to action. But who answers this call? The minutes must clearly denote which individual or committee is charged with transforming these decisions from words into reality. Is this not a clarion call to accountability, ensuring that every promise made in the spirit of advancement and growth is duly fulfilled?

---

* Jim Brown, *Effective Minutes Writing* (CharityChannel Press, 2020).

- **Maintain a Clear Timeline:** Orderliness and clarity are not just virtues but necessities in the realm of minute-keeping. Structuring the minutes to reflect a clear timeline of events offers a lens through which the progression of discussions and decisions can be viewed, imbued with context and understanding. Does this not pave the way for a future where every step taken by the organization is guided by wisdom drawn from its past?

- **Be Accessible:** In the spirit of transparency and inclusivity, the swift distribution of the minutes is essential. This ensures every stakeholder's gaze can be turned towards the collective vision, understanding the actions and decisions propelling the organization forward. Is this not a reflection of our commitment to a governance rooted in openness, where every soul invested in our cause remains informed and engaged?

In weaving the minutes with diligence, accuracy, and a profound sense of responsibility, we are not merely documenting meetings; we are crafting a legacy. We are laying down the steppingstones for future generations to walk upon, guided by the light of our present-day decisions and discussions.

This is our invitation to unlock the potential lying dormant within these written records, to live out our calling with unwavering conviction.

Let us then, with fervent hearts and minds, commit to creating minutes that not only recount our meetings but resonate with the essence of our mission and ministry.

Adjournment and Follow Through

As the chapter of a meeting comes to an end, are we not called to pause and ponder the steps that lead from deliberation to divine action? Adjournment is not merely a procedural formality; it is a moment of commitment, a time to ensure that the seeds of discussion sown in the fertile ground of collective wisdom are ready to be nurtured into fruition.

Adjournment - A Sacred Seal: The role of the Chairman transcends mere meeting facilitation; it embodies the stewardship of ensuring that all matters of importance have been duly addressed. Is it not paramount that before the formal closure of the meeting, there is a harmonious agreement on the action items crafted within? Confirming the next rendezvous of minds and hearts ensures the continuity of our mission. Is this not a sacred seal on the covenant we share as stewards of our cause?

Follow-Through - The Heartbeat of Action: But what of the path that unfolds after the amen has been pronounced? The true testament to the power of a non-profit board meeting lies not within its convened hours, but in the echo of its impact reverberating through time. Follow-through is the heartbeat of action, the rhythm that sustains the momentum of change.

Action Plan Development - Charting the Course: How do we translate vision into victory, intention into impact? By crafting a clear action plan that delineates the what, the when, and the who, we set forth on this sacred voyage with a map in hand. Identifying tasks, assigning deadlines, and designating responsible parties transforms the ethereal into the tangible. We are architects of our future, builders of bridges between dreams and reality?

Accountability and Reporting - The Pillars of Progress: In the pursuit of our divine calling, regular follow-up and reporting stand as the pillars of progress, the guardians of accountability. This cycle of reflection and communication allows for the navigation of our course, adjusting the sails as the winds of circumstance and insight dictate. This is how we honor our commitment to those we serve, by ensuring that our actions align with our aspirations?

Continuous Improvement - The Journey of Excellence: The quest for operational excellence is a perpetual journey, not a destination. With each meeting, we are bestowed the opportunity to reflect, to learn, and to evolve. Seeking feedback from board members is like gathering manna in the wilderness; it nourishes our mission, empowering us to stride forward with renewed purpose and passion.

By weaving these elements into the tapestry of our meetings, non-profit organizations can ascend to new heights of governance and service. The board meeting, then, becomes more than a mechanism of administration; it transforms into a crucible of change, a beacon of hope in the noble pursuit of philanthropy. Harness its potential, unlock your potential, and watch as intention blossoms into effective action, guiding your organization towards its God-given destiny.

The Need

Non-profit board meetings are critical for steering an organization towards success, and effective leadership is essential in ensuring these meetings are productive. By embodying qualities of clarity, diplomacy, strategic thinking, and efficient meeting management, the Chairman sets the tone for a successful board meeting.

Incorporating Robert's Rules of Order and crafting a well-structured agenda with accurate minutes are key components in running an effective meeting. And most importantly, following through on decisions made during the meeting ensures that progress is being made towards achieving the organization's mission. With these elements in place, non-profit board meetings can truly be a catalyst for positive change and impact within the community.

So, it is important for the Chairman to continuously strive for improvement in their leadership skills and adapt to the changing needs of the organization and its members. By doing so, they can guide their board towards making informed decisions and driving meaningful progress in pursuit of their organization's goals.

Although the Chairman's role is crucial in facilitating productive board meetings, it is also important for all members to contribute actively and work together towards the betterment of the organization. With a strong and well-functioning board, non-profit organizations can truly make a difference in their communities and achieve their mission with success.

Chapter 8

Non-Profit Management Styles

Today's non-profit organizations stand as beacons of hope, demonstrating the incredible power of flexibility, innovation, and a steadfast commitment to their mission. These attributes are not just essential; they are the lifeblood of successful philanthropic endeavors. But, have you paused to reflect on the profound impact this approach could have on your personal and professional growth? How often do we truly consider our work as a platform for ministry?

We acknowledge the dynamic landscape of non-profit management and its unique challenges. Yet, we see these challenges as opportunities—opportunities to innovate, to adapt, and to truly make a difference in the world. It's time to ask ourselves, how can we contribute to this noble cause? How can we use our skills, our resources, and our energy to empower those around us and further the mission of these invaluable organizations?

- Empower
- Unlock your potential
- Live out your calling

These are not just words; they are invitations to join a movement of individuals dedicated to making a significant impact through their work. By integrating the values of our faith with our professional endeavors, we create a synergy that not only enhances our effectiveness but also enriches our lives and those of others.

Flexibility is Key

Flexibility is a crucial characteristic for any non-profit manager. The nature of non-profit work often involves dealing with unexpected challenges and constantly adapting to new situations. This requires managers to be open-minded, able to think on their feet, and willing to adjust plans and strategies as needed.

In the non-profit world, things rarely go according to plan. Funding may fall through, key team members may leave unexpectedly, or external factors may impact the organization's ability to carry out its mission. In these situations, it is essential for non-profit managers to be flexible and able to pivot quickly. This ensures that the organization can continue moving forward and making a positive impact.

Innovation Drives Success: Innovation is another crucial aspect of effective non-profit management. Non-profits must constantly find new ways to address social or environmental issues and achieve their goals. This requires managers to think creatively and be open to new ideas and approaches.

Innovative management allows non-profits to stay relevant, engage donors and volunteers, and make a greater impact in their communities. By continuously seeking out new solutions and approaches, non-profit managers can identify more effective ways to address issues and reach their goals.

Mission-Driven Management: At the core of every successful non-profit is a strong mission and purpose that guides all decision-making. Non-profit managers must keep this mission at the forefront of their minds and ensure that it aligns with all organizational practices.

A clearly defined mission can inspire passion, dedication, and motivation in both staff members and supporters. It also serves as a benchmark for success and helps non-profits stay focused on their ultimate goal.

Several Non-Profit Management Styles

Non-profit organizations thrive on diversity, not just in their causes but also in how they're managed. Understanding and implementing the right management style can significantly boost your team's morale, efficiency, and overall impact. Here are several non-profit management styles that can inspire and drive your organization to greater heights:

- **Transformational Leadership:** This leadership style is all about inspiring and motivating team members to exceed their own expectations and significantly contribute to the organization's goals. Transformational leaders are not just visionaries; they also foster a culture of trust, creativity, and innovation, engaging with their team in a way that encourages them to dream bigger and achieve more than they thought possible. They are adept at recognizing the potential in others and unlocking it.

- **Servant Leadership:** Characterized by putting the needs of employees, beneficiaries, and the community first, servant leadership focuses on the growth and well-being of individuals and the communities to which they belong. This approach does more than just lead; it builds a strong, supportive base capable of taking on any challenge with enthusiasm and dedication. Servant leaders prioritize their team's needs over their own, fostering an environment of care and commitment.

- **Democratic Leadership:** This leadership style is marked by shared decision-making among management and team members, promoting a deep sense of belonging and accountability within the group. By actively involving team members in the decision-making process, democratic leadership not only encourages active participation but also leverages diverse viewpoints for better, more inclusive outcomes. It's a collaborative approach that values each member's input.

- **Laissez-Faire Leadership:** Ideal for teams comprised of highly skilled, self-motivated individuals, the laissez-faire approach allows team members considerable freedom to innovate and make decisions on their own. This style is most effective when the leader provides the necessary resources and support without micromanaging, trusting in the team's expertise and abilities to lead their own work effectively.

- **Situational Leadership:** Recognizing that no single leadership style is suitable for all scenarios, situational leaders dynamically adapt their approach based on the specific task at hand, the team's current needs, and the immediate goals. This flexibility ensures that leadership is always optimally aligned with the organization's current demands and objectives, making it a highly responsive and effective leadership style.

- **Coaching Leadership:** Focused squarely on developing individuals to reach their full potential, coaching leaders work closely with team members to set goals, offer constructive feedback, and provide mentorship. It's a style particularly effective in organizations, such as non-profits, aiming to build strong future leaders from within by fostering a culture of personal and professional growth.

- **Collaborative Leadership:** Understanding that complex problems require the collective efforts of diverse groups, collaborative leaders actively work across organizational boundaries to bring people together. This leadership style leverages partnerships, coalitions, and networking to achieve shared goals. In the interconnected world of non-profits, collaborative leadership is invaluable in tackling broad issues through unified efforts, making it especially effective for achieving widespread impact.

Each of these management styles offers unique advantages and can be tailored to suit your non-profit's mission, culture, and challenges. Remember, the most successful non-profit managers often blend elements from different styles to create a dynamic, responsive leadership approach that drives their organization forward with passion and purpose. Be bold, be innovative, and, most importantly, be mission-driven. Your cause deserves nothing less!

Volunteers Matter

Have you ever paused to consider the incredible power of an offering not measured in currency, but in time? Volunteers are indeed the unsung heroes, the divine force that breathes life into our ministries. They step forward not for monetary reward, but for the opportunity to be part of something greater than themselves—a chance to weave their thread into the larger tapestry of our shared vision.

In this spirit, how could we not treasure and honor these generous souls? Recognizing the invaluable contributions of our volunteers means more than a simple thank you. It's about respecting their time, empowering them with the same dedication we extend to our officers, and investing in their growth through continuous learning and recognition.

But why does this matter so profoundly? When a volunteer feels truly seen and valued, they transform. They become passionate advocates for our cause, carrying the message forward with the fervency of those who have witnessed the truth firsthand. This powerful transformation not only enriches their own spiritual and professional journeys but amplifies the impact of our ministry far beyond what we could achieve alone.

This is not merely a suggestion—it's a plea to recognize the heart and soul of our missions. For in valuing our volunteers, we are indeed valuing the very essence of humanity and faith itself. Join us in celebrating and uplifting these extraordinary individuals who choose to serve, for they are the key to unlocking our collective potential and achieving greatness beyond measure.

In conclusion, navigating the vast terrain of non-profit management demands a nuanced understanding of the various leadership styles that inspire and mobilize people towards a common goal. From transformational leaders who ignite passion and drive vision, to servant leaders who place the welfare of others at the forefront of their mission, the art of leadership within non-profits is both complex and profoundly impactful. It requires a delicate balance between guiding and empowering, between inspiring and serving. The styles discussed here offer a framework for effective leadership but stepping into these roles with authenticity and purpose is what truly makes a difference.

As you reflect on these leadership styles, consider how they align with your personal values, your organization's culture, and the unique challenges you face. The most effective leaders are those who adapt, learn, and continually evolve their approach to meet the needs of their teams and the communities they serve. Remember, at the heart of non-profit work is a mission fueled by passion and a vision for a better world. Whether you're leading with a coaching mindset, fostering collaboration, or empowering through a democratic approach, your leadership can light the path to achieving remarkable outcomes.

Embrace the opportunity to make a profound impact. Lead with conviction, compassion, and courage, knowing that your leadership style isn't just about managing tasks—it's about transforming lives and making the world a better place. The future of non-profit leadership is bright, and it starts with you.

Chapter 9

HR Strategies for Faith-Based Organizations

In the sacred symphony of work and worship, faith doesn't merely echo through the halls of corporate ladders; it resonates in the heartbeats of every employee dedicated to a higher calling. For non-profits, where faith is not just a value but the very foundation, Human Resources (HR) management becomes a ministry—an art form that empowers, engages, and echoes the organizational mission with every employment decision made.

When your goal transcends profit to touch lives and transform communities, your HR strategy must reflect this divine mission. Here, we will explore how to craft an HR approach that serves as a bridge between the spiritual and the professional, ensuring that your organization's compassionate core is mirrored in its people practices.

Finding 'Servant Leaders'

Are you on a quest to find more than just an employee, but a *servant leader* whose professional prowess is matched only by their heart for service? Imagine the power of combining your organization's mission with the passion and dedication of someone who sees their work not just as a job, but as a calling. This is not just recruitment; it's a call to action for those ready to serve with excellence and lead with humility. But the question arises, where does one start such a noble pursuit?

In the realm of non-profit organizations, the process of recruitment transcends the mere alignment of qualifications with job descriptions. It's about seeking out those rare gems—individuals who embody the essence of servant leadership. These are the people who understand that their professional achievements are not the end goal but a means to contribute to something greater than themselves. How, then, can we unlock the door to this vast pool of potential servant leaders? Where do we begin our search for these paragons of service and leadership?

The answer lies in looking beyond the resume, in seeking out those whose lives are a testament to their commitment to service. It involves creating spaces where the values of ministry and business converge, empowering individuals to live out their calling in every aspect of their lives. The recruiter must ask themself, "Am I prepared to empower, to unlock potential, and to mentor those who are ready to step into their calling with courage and faith?"

Remember, the quest for servant leaders is not just about finding someone to fill a position. It's about identifying those who will carry forward the torch of your mission with zeal and unwavering commitment. It's a call to those ready to empower and be empowered, to unlock their potential, and to live out their calling in the service of others.

Casting the Vision

Before setting out on your quest, it's pivotal to forge a crystal-clear vision of the ideal team member you seek. What virtues should illuminate their character? Is their heart marked by humility, yet their spirit adorned with the courage to serve? Are they the torchbearers of your mission, illuminating every path they tread? Sculpting this vision is more than a preparatory step; it's ensuring that each soul you welcome aboard resonates with the core essence of your cause—a binding purpose that echoes far beyond the confines of an interview room.

Think of this not just as recruitment but as a calling. You're not merely filling a position; you're inviting someone to join a crusade. Can you see them? Those vibrant souls, humble yet fearless, ready to champion your cause with every fiber of their being. This, dear reader, is the essence of casting a vision. It's about envisioning a future where every new recruit not only aligns with but amplifies the spirit of your mission.

The Art of Storytelling

Recruitment in the realm of non-profits transcends traditional boundaries—it's a narrative woven with the threads of human experience. It's about crafting tales that echo the transformation ignited by your endeavors. These stories, brimming with life and change, beckon the kind-hearted and the competent. Narrate the journeys of those touched not just by the work but by the enveloping aura of collaboration and compassion. Share these powerful testimonials and watch as your candidates become eager to author their chapter in this grand narrative.

Remember, storytelling is not just a strategy; it's a beacon.

It lights up the path for those seeking to make a difference, guiding them to your door. In the tapestry of non-profit recruitment, each testimony, each shared experience, is a thread that draws the right hearts closer to your mission. Are you prepared to wield the power of storytelling to inspire, to ignite passion, and to gather a community of servant leaders around your cause?

Addressing Ambiguity with Clarity

In the world of Human Resources, clarity isn't just kindness; in the sphere of non-profits, it ascends to the realm of respect. Being transparent about roles, remunerations, benefits, and the structure of your organization isn't just procedure—it's building trust, the very foundation upon which the sanctum of non-profit HR stands. When potential recruits grasp the full spectrum of their role and rewards in serving your mission, their commitment deepens, rooted in understanding and conviction.

This clarity is your beacon of respect and trust. It's an invitation extended to those considering joining your ranks—an assurance that their dedication to the cause is met with honesty and openness. Are you ready to clear the haze, to offer a lens of transparency that transforms uncertainty into commitment? This is more than mere HR practice; it's a covenant of trust between you and those poised to dedicate their lives to the vision you've cast.

In every step of this sacred quest—to cast the vision, to weave the narrative, to clarify the path—remember, you're not just recruiting; you're gathering a fellowship of believers, ready to serve, ready to transform the world with you. Welcome to the magnificent journey of creating a legacy through the hearts you choose to bring along.

Nurturing a Culture of Continual Growth

Creating a culture of growth and development within non-profit organizations is like preparing fertile land for an abundant harvest. It's a labor fueled by dedication and love, promising a rich yield of progress and transformation. But one might wonder, how does Human Resources spearhead this crucial initiative?

In the heart of every thriving non-profit lies a commitment to nurturing its most valuable asset—its people. Just as a farmer tends to each plant, ensuring it receives enough sunlight, water, and nutrients, Human Resources plays a pivotal role in fostering an environment where every team member can flourish. This involves more than mere administrative tasks; it's about cultivating a space where individuals are empowered, their potentials unlocked, and their callings passionately pursued.

But what does it truly mean to "empower" and "unlock potential"? How can one "live out a calling" in the non-profit sector? These aren't just lofty ideals; they're actionable pathways. Empowering your team means providing them with the tools, knowledge, and opportunities to grow both professionally and personally. To unlock someone's potential is to recognize and nurture their unique talents and skills, guiding them to use these gifts in service of a greater mission. Living out a calling, then, becomes the natural outcome of this nurturing process—a synthesis of personal fulfillment and professional achievement in the pursuit of a shared vision.

Human Resources leads this charge by implementing strategies that align with the core values of ministry and service. From tailored training programs and leadership development workshops to creating open channels for feedback and collaboration, HR's role is multifaceted. Each initiative is a seed planted, promising a future where employees not only achieve their best work but also find deeper meaning and satisfaction in their roles.

The question then becomes, are you ready to transform your organization into a greenhouse of growth and fulfillment? Are you prepared to lead with faith, intertwining the principles of business and ministry to create an unstoppable force for good? This is not just about professional development; it's a holistic approach to living out one's faith through their work, turning every task, every project, and every challenge into an opportunity for ministry.

By fostering a culture of development, Human Resources doesn't just lead a growth initiative; they lay the groundwork for a movement. A movement that sees each employee not just as a worker, but as a vital part of a living, breathing mission. A mission that transcends the boundaries of the workplace, reaching into the heart of the community and beyond.

The Mentorship Matrix

Imagine unlocking the full potential of your team through the power of mentorship. Envision a place where experienced employees don't just pass on skills but also share the profound wisdom of your organization's culture and values. How powerful would it be to pair new recruits with mentors, creating not just a working relationship but a community bonded by mutual learning and shared journeys? This is the essence of the Mentorship Matrix—where connections forge stronger teams and enrich learning experiences.

Educational Partnerships

Now, imagine extending your reach beyond the confines of

your organization to collaborate with educational institutions. Picture creating bespoke programs tailored to the unique needs of your mission, where formal and informal learning pathways shepherd your employees toward both professional excellence and spiritual growth. These partnerships are not just about skill enhancement; they're opportunities to infuse your team with diverse perspectives, revitalizing your non-profit's approach with fresh insight and energy.

What could be more inspiring than watching your team grow, equipped with knowledge and skills that align perfectly with your mission? It's about opening doors to continuous learning and development, guided by a shared vision of service and ministry.

The Culture of Feedback

Cultivating a culture where feedback is exchanged freely and constructively is one of the main building blocks of success. Imagine performance appraisals that, while challenging, are approached with grace and serve as milestones for growth and recognition. Think about the impact of constructive criticism, balanced with praise for effort, inspiring each employee to reach new heights and see their role's value in the grand tapestry of your shared mission.

How revolutionary would it be to create an environment where feedback is not feared but welcomed as a tool for empowerment and affirmation? It's about building a culture where every voice is heard, every contribution valued, and every step forward celebrated. Are you prepared to foster such a culture, where feedback becomes the wind beneath the wings of your team, elevating them toward their highest calling in both their professional and spiritual lives?

. . .

In weaving together the Mentorship Matrix, Educational Partnerships, and The Culture of Feedback, you're not just implementing strategies; you're igniting a movement. A movement that champions growth, nurtures potential, and celebrates every individual's journey toward living out their calling. Are you ready to lead this charge, inspiring your team to unlock their fullest potential and transform the world around them with faith, passion, and purpose?

Retention Strategies as Testaments of Trust

Retention within non-profit organizations is not just about keeping employees; it's a testament to trust—a sacred reciprocity that binds the heart of the organization to its devoted stewards. How, then, does one cultivate and nurture this profound trust that anchors our team members firmly to the cause we hold dear?

Trust is the bedrock upon which the pillars of any successful non-profit stand. It's the unwavering faith each team member places in the organization, believing in its mission, its values, and its leadership. But how does one go about creating such a resilient bond? How do we ensure that this trust not only takes root but flourishes, blossoming into a lasting commitment?

The answer lies in recognizing the immense value of each individual's contribution. It's about affirming their role not just as employees but as integral messengers of the mission. By empowering them, acknowledging their efforts, and investing in their growth, we not only unlock their potential but also solidify their connection to the cause.

Imagine creating an environment where every team member feels seen, heard, and valued. Where their contributions are not just acknowledged but celebrated. Isn't this the essence of building trust? When people know that they matter, that their work has purpose, and that they are part of a larger vision, they are inspired to stay and contribute even more passionately.

> Empowerment
>
> Recognition
>
> Investment

...these are not mere buzzwords but the very pillars upon which trust is built. When we empower our team members to unlock their fullest potential, when we recognize their hard work and dedication, and when we invest in their professional and spiritual growth, we are sending a powerful message. We are telling them, "You are valued. You are essential to our mission. Together, we can make a difference."

But the question that beckons is, are you ready to take these steps? Are you prepared to build a culture where trust thrives, where every team member feels empowered to live out their calling, and where the mission becomes a shared heartbeat?

This is not just about retention. It's about forging a legacy of trust and commitment, of faith and purpose. It's about creating a family united by a common cause, ready to face any challenge with faith and determination. It's about leading with vision, inspiring with passion, and building a foundation of trust that will endure for generations to come?

Recognizing Contributions Publicly

Public acknowledgment of an employee's hard work is a beacon of light on the often-strenuous path of service and sacrifice. Isn't it true that such recognition transforms their role from being just a job to becoming a celebrated chapter in a much grander, virtuous narrative? Imagine the profound impact when one's labor is not only appreciated but heralded as a vital piece of the mission's success. How empowering is it to know that your contributions are seen, valued, and honored publicly?

This act of recognition serves more than just to applaud; it acts as a shield against the creeping shadows of disillusionment. It sends a powerful message: "Your efforts matter. You are an essential part of this mission." Isn't this exactly what fuels our hearts with courage and our spirits with determination to press on, even when the road gets tough?

Flexibility as an Indicator of Empathy

In the realm of non-profit work, where service transcends the conventional boundaries of time and space, how crucial is flexibility? Offering flexibility is not merely a strategy for retention; it is a profound expression of empathy. This understanding that sometimes, life's demands stretch beyond the confines of the cubicle or the clock, speaks volumes of an organization's heart for its people.

Think about it—when you accommodate the ebb and flow of your team members' lives outside work, aren't you applying the very essence of ministry into your management practices? This gesture of empathy is like a balm to the weary spirit, a testament to the organization's commitment to serve not just the community but also those who shoulder the mission. Is there a more beautiful way to embody the spirit of service than by showing empathy to your own team?

Creating Inclusive Rituals

Why limit the power of rituals and traditions to religious observances when they can be woven into the very fabric of your organization? Instituting inclusive gatherings and celebrations that honor our faith and backgrounds is like weaving threads of unity and belonging into the tapestry of your organization. These rituals become the connective tissues that bind your team, strengthening relationships, fostering loyalty, and enhancing retention.

Imagine the beauty of an organization where everyone feels included, valued, and connected—not just by shared goals but by shared experiences that celebrate the rich mosaic of humanity within your team. Isn't this the epitome of building a community? In creating these inclusive spaces, you reinforce a sense of belonging and shared purpose, essential pillars for a team that's not just working together but thriving together in faith, service, and mission.

In weaving together public recognition, empathetic flexibility, and inclusive rituals, you're not just employing strategies for retention. You are nurturing a culture where every individual is empowered to unlock their potential, live out their calling, and contribute to a mission that transcends the ordinary. Are you ready to lead with vision, inspire with passion, and create an environment where every team member can soar to new heights, both professionally and spiritually?

Stepping Into The Ministry of HR

At the heart of non-profit HR lies the belief that every employment decision is a covenant—a commitment to the organizational calling. The strategies we've discussed are tools to foster this covenant, but remember, the essence of ministry in the workplace is in the daily, deliberate, and devoted actions of the HR team and the entire workforce.

Integrate prayer and reflection in your hiring processes, in your development plans, and in your ways of retention. Non-profit HR, when threaded with the spiritual thread, not only strengthens the organization but also becomes the conduit through which the ministry of service and transformation flows freely, tirelessly, and gracefully.

Non-profits hold the formidable and fortuitous position of marrying business acumen with spiritual grace. It's a balancing act that, when performed with integrity and intention, births miracles in the form of empowered and impassioned employees who embody the ministry of the workplace.

In this noble isle where faith and work meet, may your HR practices be the sermons that inspire and the songs that soar. May they reflect the miracles your non-profit seeks to manifest in the world. The ministry of HR in non-profits is not just about managing resources; it's about maximizing the individual and collective potential to manifest a higher purpose. It's about transforming lives, starting from within. Welcome, then, to the ministry of your workplace. Your calling awaits—embrace it, champion it, and live it out with fervor and faith.

In the dynamic world of faith-based organizations, the Human Resources department is not just an administrative function; it is the heart of cultivating a culture where faith, purpose, and work intersect to create something extraordinary. The strategies of recognizing contributions, offering flexibility, and creating inclusive rituals are not mere policies but are acts of ministry that reflect the organization's core values and beliefs. These practices empower individuals and teams to perform their best, knowing they are valued, understood, and part of a mission much greater than themselves.

This chapter has been a call to action for HR professionals and leaders within faith-based organizations to envisage and realize a workplace where every individual is nurtured, celebrated, and given the opportunity to thrive. By integrating these HR strategies, organizations can transcend traditional management approaches, fostering a work environment infused with purpose, passion, and spirit.

As we conclude, remember that the true essence of HR in faith-based organizations lies in its ability to weave together the individual threads of each employee's talents, beliefs, and aspirations into a vibrant tapestry that illustrates the organization's mission. It's about leading not just with strategies but with heart, vision, and an unwavering faith in the potential of your team to make a difference in the world.

The ministry of HR is a profound calling, an opportunity to serve, inspire, and lead in ways that honor both organizational goals and divine purpose. May your journey be filled with the joy of discovery, the fulfillment of meaningful achievements, and the profound satisfaction of contributing to a cause far greater than any one person. In your hands lies the power to not only shape careers but to transform lives. Stand proud in this knowledge, for you are not just HR professionals; you are guardians of the faith, shepherds of your organization's most precious resource—its people.

Chapter 10

The Path to Non-Profit Sustainability

Crafting a resilient future for non-profit organizations hinges on ingenuity and adaptability. At the intersection of philanthropy and business lies social entrepreneurship – a potent force for sustainability in the non-profit sector. Here we explore how social entrepreneurship can invigorate your non-profit's mission, drawing a blueprint for longevity and impact. Join us on an enlightening exploration of strategies tailored to those steering the course of non-profit ships, boiling down challenges into actionable solutions.

Understanding the Current Landscape

Non-profits have long been pillars of service, operating within a regulatory and social framework that values their contribution to the greater good. However, as the global socio-economic narrative evolves, non-profits find themselves challenged by resource scarcity, increased competition for funding, and the growing complexity of the societal ills they seek to address.

These dynamics underscore the need for a more sustainable approach that moves beyond traditional grant-based models. Financial volatility is a reality that cannot be ignored, especially for non-profit organizations that primarily depend on donations and grants. This dependence can lead to uncertainty, making it challenging to plan and execute long-term strategies effectively. However, have you considered this not as a setback, but as a call to action? A call to empower and innovate in the face of adversity? By diversifying revenue streams, not only can non-profits mitigate these financial risks, but they can also amplify their impact. Yet, this diversification must not come at the cost of the organization's soul. Every step forward, every new venture, must align with the mission that beats at the heart of the organization.

In understanding the current landscape, non-profit leaders must internalize the following factors:

- **Financial Volatility**: Depending solely on donations and grants for funding places non-profit organizations in a vulnerable position, subjecting them to financial volatility. This instability can severely hinder their ability to plan and execute long-term strategies effectively. By diversifying revenue streams—such as incorporating social enterprises, membership fees, or selling branded merchandise—non-profits can mitigate these financial risks. This not only provides a more stable financial foundation but also enables them to maximize their impact over time.

- **Competition for Funding**: In the growing landscape of non-profit organizations, there's a noticeable surge in competition for funding. This uptick means that organizations must now go the extra mile to differentiate themselves from the crowd. It's essential for them to clearly articulate and showcase their unique value proposition, demonstrating to potential donors and investors exactly why they stand out. This strategic differentiation is crucial in capturing the attention and support of those looking to invest in meaningful causes.

- **Growing Complexity of Societal Issues**: In today's rapidly changing world, societal issues are becoming increasingly complex and multifaceted. This complexity demands that non-profit organizations not only keep pace but also lead the way in innovation and adaptation to maintain their effectiveness in achieving their missions. Social entrepreneurship offers a dynamic framework that encourages this level of agility and innovation. Through its principles, non-profits can pioneer new strategies, develop innovative solutions, and adapt to the evolving landscape of societal needs, ensuring they can continue to make a meaningful impact.

- **Mission Alignment**: Expanding and diversifying revenue streams is essential for financial resilience; however, it's paramount that these efforts do not dilute the organization's mission. Any strategy employed must maintain a strong alignment with the organization's core purpose, ensuring that growth and diversification enhance rather than distract from the mission.

- **Innovation as an Imperative**: In today's ever-increasing culture, innovation is not just a nice-to-have; it's a necessity. Non-profit organizations must develop innovative responses that are not only effective in addressing current challenges but are also scalable and replicable across different contexts. Such innovation ensures the sector remains relevant and capable of meeting the evolving needs of the communities it serves.

The path to non-profit sustainability is both a challenge and an opportunity—an invitation to rethink, reimagine, and revolutionize the way we approach social good. By embracing financial diversification, fostering strategic differentiation, tackling complex societal issues with innovative solutions, and ensuring that every step taken aligns with the core mission, non-profits can secure a more stable and impactful future.

It's time to view the hurdles not as obstacles but as catalysts for growth and transformation. By adopting social entrepreneurship principles, non-profits can rise to meet the demands of an ever-evolving world, ensuring their invaluable contributions continue to resonate across communities and generations. The future is bright for those who dare to innovate, adapt, and inspire.

The Rise of Social Entrepreneurship

In the vibrant landscape of today's world, social entrepreneurship emerges as a revolutionary approach that blends the rigor of business with the heart of solving societal challenges. It stands on the powerful idea that efficiency, scalability, and sustainability are not just corporate buzzwords but are essential tools for transforming how non-profits function. This concept energizes the spirit of innovation, urging us to rethink the foundations of charity and philanthropy.

Have you ever considered the profound impact of applying business principles to address social issues? Social entrepreneurship does precisely that—it's a call to action that invites us to empower communities and create economic ecosystems that align with our deepest values. It's about challenging outdated notions and daring to envision a world where non-profits aren't just surviving but thriving through strategic, sustainable practices.

Case Study
MULLY

Imagine a world where a single person's vision transforms the lives of thousands, where despair turns into hope, and where challenges evolve into opportunities. This is not a mere daydream, but the real-life story of Charles Mully, a Kenyan entrepreneur-turned-philanthropist who founded the MULLY Children's Family (MCF). Mully's personal commitment to change the lives of orphaned children across Africa serves as an unparalleled example of social entrepreneurship in action.

Born into poverty, Mully overcame insurmountable odds to become a successful businessman. However, his life took a dramatic turn when he decided to devote his wealth and resources to create a sanctuary for the destitute and orphaned. The MCF, born out of this vision, is not just an orphanage; it's an ecosystem of change. It provides children with shelter, education, healthcare, and, most importantly, love. But Mully didn't stop there; he integrated innovative agricultural projects, clean water initiatives, and renewable energy sources to ensure sustainability and self-sufficiency.

The MCF is a testament to what can be achieved when

compassion meets innovation. It showcases how social entrepreneurship can build bridges between communities and generate sustainable solutions to social issues. Charles Mully's narrative is not just a case study; it's a beacon of hope. It urges us not just to dream of a better world but to take actionable steps towards creating it. Through the lens of Mully's life, we are reminded that every challenge we face is an opportunity to make a difference, to innovate, and to transform lives.

To learn more about the incredible journey of Charles Mully and the transformative work of the MULLY Children's Family, I encourage you to explore their official website at Mully Children's Family.* This platform offers an in-depth look at their initiatives, from groundbreaking agricultural projects to their renewable energy ventures, and how you can support or become part of this life-changing mission.

Additionally, the documentary *"Mully"*, available on various streaming services, provides a captivating and detailed narrative of Charles Mully's life and the genesis of MCF. This film shines a light on the obstacles encountered and the profound influence of an individual born into poverty who decided to transcend their humble beginnings by blending compassion with innovation. Whether you're moved by the power of individual action or looking to support sustainable solutions to societal issues, the story of Mully and MCF is a compelling testament to the difference one person can make.

YOU Can Do It Too!

What does this mean for you and me? If MULLY can do it, so can we! How can we contribute to this dynamic shift towards impactful change? This is where the power of faith

---

* www.mullychildrensfamily.org

and purpose intertwines with our professional aspirations, guiding us toward a path of meaningful work. The essence of social entrepreneurship is not merely in its ability to solve problems but in its capacity to inspire individuals to unlock their potential and live out their calling in ways that enrich both society and the soul.

Imagine a world where every business move, every strategy, and every innovation serves a greater purpose. This is the heart of social entrepreneurship—creating value that transcends profit, uplifting communities, and paving the way for a brighter future. It's a testament to human ingenuity and compassion, proving that when we align our work with our beliefs, extraordinary transformation is possible.

Key Tenets of Social Entrepreneurship

- **Innovative Revenue Models:** Non-profit organizations are increasingly exploring and adopting innovative business models that not only generate income but also further their charitable objectives. These models vary widely, from fee-for-service models, where services are provided for a fee, to cause-related marketing, where they partner with companies to receive a portion of the proceeds from sales of certain products. This approach allows them to diversify their funding sources and become more financially sustainable.

- **Cross-Sector Collaboration:** Social entrepreneurship thrives on the fertile ground of collaboration across different sectors. Non-profits are actively partnering with for-profit entities and governmental agencies to orchestrate synergies that significantly magnify their impact. These partnerships can range from simple cooperation agreements to complex joint ventures, leveraging the strengths of each sector to tackle social issues more effectively.

- **Impact Measurement and Reporting:** A rigorous and systematic approach to measuring and reporting the impact of their activities is a hallmark of modern social entrepreneurship. This ensures accountability and transparency, which in turn resonate with funders, stakeholders, and the wider community. By using metrics and indicators, social entrepreneurs can demonstrate the effectiveness of their interventions, making a compelling case for the support of their initiatives. This focus on impact measurement emphasizes the importance of results and outcomes over inputs and activities, aligning the interests of all stakeholders around the social value created.

The rise of social entrepreneurship marks a pivotal moment in our history, stirring a powerful wave of innovation and compassion. The stories of Charles Mully and countless other social entrepreneurs illuminate a path of possibility and purpose for us all. They epitomize the essence of transforming personal convictions into global solutions, proving that individual actions, fueled by vision and compassion, can indeed reshape our world.

Now more than ever, we are called upon to harness our collective talents and energies to contribute towards a sustainable and equitable future. Whether through supporting initiatives like the MULLY Children's Family, engaging in our communities, or pioneering ventures that bridge the gap between profit and purpose, each of us holds the key to a ripple effect of positive change.

As we stand on the brink of this new era, our challenge is to rethink traditional paradigms of business and philanthropy, stepping boldly into roles that blend economic success with social impact. The narrative of social entrepreneurship is not just a hopeful story; it's a roadmap for action and an invitation for each one of us to be part of this transformative movement.

The future of social entrepreneurship—and indeed, the future of our global community—rests in the power of our collective imagination and our willingness to act. Together, we can forge a legacy of innovation, inclusion, and inspiration for generations to come.

Championing Sustainability Through Innovation

Innovation is the lifeblood of social entrepreneurship, and it finds myriad applications in ensuring the sustainability of non-profits. Innovation is the driving force behind meaningful change, and it holds the key to unlocking a treasure trove of opportunities for non-profits. But what does this look like in practice? How can leaders harness the power of innovation to not only sustain but also amplify their impact?

Imagine transforming challenges into steppingstones, leveraging technology to bridge gaps, and creating models that ensure not merely the survival but the thriving of your organization. This is the essence of innovation within the realm of social entrepreneurship—a realm where every initiative and every breakthrough paves the way for a more sustainable future.

But why stop at imagining? The path to sustainability is paved with actionable strategies that are as diverse as they are impactful. Picture integrating renewable energy solutions to reduce operational costs or employing digital platforms to widen your reach. Consider the vast potential of social media to engage communities, inspire action, and rally support for your cause. The possibilities are endless, and they all share a common thread—innovation.

Yet, this journey towards sustainability and impact isn't just about adopting new technologies or methodologies; it's about fostering a mindset of continuous improvement, creativity, and resilience. It's about leaders asking themselves the hard questions, daring to dream big, and then taking the bold steps necessary to turn those dreams into reality.

We've all heard it said,

"Where there's a will, there's a way."

In the realm of social entrepreneurship, we can take this a step further and say,

"Where there's innovation, there's a way."

As we look towards the future, let us embrace our role as champions of sustainability through innovation, leading by example and inspiring others to join us on this journey. Together, we can build a brighter future for all.

Remember, the power to champion sustainability through innovation rests in our hands. The question is, will we rise to the occasion? Will we be the beacon of change that guides our organization towards a brighter, more sustainable future?

The time to answer this call is now. Together, empowered by faith and driven by a shared vision, we can transform our world one innovative step at a time.

"Leaders don't make excuses, they make a difference."

We will examine several innovative strategies non-profit leaders can implement to bolster their organizations.

Diversifying Revenue Streams

The adage "don't put all your eggs in one basket" rings especially true for non-profits. Diversification mitigates risk and supports robust financial health. Exploration of revenue streams beyond traditional donations can encompass:

Product Sales: Developing and selling products that resonate with the non-profit's core mission can open a lucrative revenue stream. This approach might encompass a range of items such as branded merchandise, books, educational materials, and even specialty goods that directly reflect the values and goals of the organization. Crafting these products with care ensures they not only generate income but also spread awareness of the non-profit's cause.

Social Enterprise Initiatives: Launching ventures that align closely with the organization's mission, for example, green energy enterprises, job training programs for underprivileged communities, or sustainable agriculture projects, can provide a steady and sustainable source of funding. These initiatives double as practical applications of the non-profit's objectives, making a tangible difference while also contributing financially to the organization's goals.

Partnerships and Collaborations: Forging strategic alliances with businesses, educational institutions, or other non-profits can unlock new revenue streams and significantly broaden the reach and impact of the organization. These partnerships might involve co-developing products, educational programs, or community initiatives that benefit all parties involved. Collaborations not only provide financial benefits but also enhance the organization's credibility and access to resources, amplifying its ability to make a positive impact.

In essence, diversifying revenue streams isn't just a strategy—it's a necessity for the survival and prosperity of non-profits in today's dynamic world. By broadening financial foundations through product sales, social enterprise, and strategic partnerships, organizations can weather economic uncertainties, harness new opportunities for growth, and continue their crucial work with confidence. Remember, diversification isn't simply about securing financial stability; it's about building resilience, fostering innovation, and ultimately, amplifying the impact of your mission.

As we explore this path, we're not just seeking new sources of revenue; we're pioneering new ways to drive change, touch lives, and shape a better future. The journey towards financial diversification is an invitation to re-imagine what's possible, to turn visions into ventures, and dreams into real-world solutions.

Non-Profit Creation

Case Study
The North Valley Community Church

In an audacious move that epitomizes the spirit of ministry innovation, North Valley Community Church took a bold step that would reshape not only its congregation but also the surrounding community. Faced with the growing need for a larger space to accommodate its expanding membership and multifaceted programs, the church leadership identified an unconventional solution: purchasing the anchor store in a struggling local mall.

The transformation of the former retail giant into a vibrant church center was nothing short of revolutionary. With vision and ingenuity, the once-empty shell was repurposed into a sanctuary, meeting rooms, and offices, serving as a beacon of hope and a hub of community life. But the innovation didn't stop at the church's doors.

Understanding the importance of financial sustainability and community engagement, North Valley embarked on a strategic initiative to lease out the remaining mall spaces to businesses and social enterprises. This was not just about generating income; it was about creating a symbiotic ecosystem where commerce, social services, and spiritual life could coexist and reinforce each other.

This case study is a testament to the power of ministry innovation at work. Beyond reliance on traditional offerings, North Valley Community Church leveraged creative financial models to support its vision and mission. The reimagined mall now hosts a diverse mix of tenants - from cafés and bookstores to daycare centers and tech startups - each contributing to the church's financial health and enabling it to invest in more extensive community outreach programs.

What makes this project a benchmark for ministry innovation is not just its financial success, but how it revitalized a community space, provided employment opportunities, and offered essential services to the community, all while furthering the church's mission. This model demonstrates that with creativity, faith, and a willingness to venture beyond traditional paths, churches can find sustainable ways to grow their ministries and impact their communities profoundly.

The North Valley Community Church's story is more than just a case study; it's an inspiring narrative of how vision, when coupled with innovation, can transform not only a congregation but an entire community. It challenges us to rethink the role of the church in today's society and invites us to imagine new possibilities for ministry in the 21st century.

Leveraging Technology for Non-Profit Entities

In this era where technology weaves through the fabric of our everyday lives, how can faith-based ministries harness this formidable tool to further their mission? The answer lies not in the digital devices themselves but in the empowerment, they offer, transforming challenges into opportunities for growth and outreach. Technology stands as a testament to human ingenuity, a powerful enabler in the pursuit of sustainability and impact. But how can we leverage this advantage to its fullest potential?

Consider the boundless possibilities that online fundraising presents. Have you thought about the power of engaging supporters through digital channels? This approach doesn't just widen your donor base; it revolutionizes the giving process, making it simpler, more accessible, and thereby multiplying the avenues through which blessings can flow. Imagine a world where anyone, anywhere, can support your cause with just a click—this is the world technology invites us to create.

But the power of technology extends beyond fundraising. How often have we found ourselves overwhelmed by decisions, wishing for clarity and direction? Here, technology offers a beacon of hope. Data-driven decision making, enabled by analytics and visualization tools, empowers leaders to illuminate the path ahead with informed choices about program design and resource allocation. It's about turning data into wisdom, ensuring that every decision aligns with the mission and maximizes impact.

Technological Tools for Enhancing
Faith-based Outreachs

In today's digital era, technology offers an unprecedented toolkit for faith-based organizations to amplify their outreach and deepen their impact. Here's a curated list of technological tools and inventive ways they can be integrated into your Non-Profit entity:

1. **Social Media Platforms**: Leverage the power of platforms like Facebook, Instagram, and Twitter to connect with your community, share inspirational messages, and broadcast live events. Social media is not just a broadcasting tool; it's a two-way street that invites engagement, feedback, and community building.
2. **Mobile Apps**: Developing a customized app can revolutionize the way you engage with your congregation. From daily devotionals, event schedules, to donation functionalities, a mobile app consolidates your ministry's offerings into the palm of your follower's hand, making spiritual growth resources constantly accessible.

3. **Livestreaming Services**: Platforms such as YouTube Live and Zoom allow you to livestream worship services, prayer meetings, and events, ensuring that no one misses out on spiritual nourishment because of physical barriers. Livestreaming extends your reach beyond geographical limitations, inviting a global audience into your place of worship.
4. **Online Donation Platforms**: Tools like PayPal, Stripe, and GoFundMe simplify the giving process, making it easy for supporters to contribute financially to your ministry. These platforms offer secure, hassle-free donation options for a tech-savvy generation that prefers online transactions.
5. **Email Marketing Software**: Utilize platforms like MailChimp or Constant Contact to keep your community informed and engaged. Whether it's a weekly newsletter, event announcements, or fundraising appeals, email marketing is a cost-effective way to maintain a consistent line of communication with your congregation.
6. **CRM (Customer Relationship Management) Systems**: A CRM tailored for non-profits, such as Salesforce for Nonprofits, can transform how you manage relationships with your congregation and donors. These systems enable you to track interactions, understand community needs better, and personalize your outreach efforts.
7. **Content Management Systems (CMS)**: A robust CMS for your website, like WordPress, allows you to easily publish content, sermons, and updates, maintain an active blog, and provide

resources for spiritual growth. Your website is often the first port of call for those exploring faith or looking for a church home, making it a critical tool in your outreach arsenal.

8. **Project Management Tools**: Platforms like Trello, Slack, and Asana can streamline the planning and execution of community projects and events. By enhancing team collaboration and task management, these tools ensure that your ministry can carry out its vision with efficiency and grace.

9. **Personal Ministry Websites:** As leaders a personal website can serve as a powerful tool for sharing your testimony, teachings, and spiritual insights. It's an avenue to connect with a wider audience and inspire others through your journey of faith.

10. **Virtual Reality (VR) Technology:** As technology continues to evolve, we see the potential for VR technology to enhance spiritual experiences. Imagine virtual reality tours of biblical sites or immersive worship experiences that transport individuals into a sacred space, regardless of their physical location.

By adopting these technological tools, faith-based organizations can not only broaden their reach but also deepen their connection with individuals seeking spiritual guidance. The key is to view technology not as a replacement for traditional ministry methods, but as a complement that enriches and expands the ability to fulfill your mission in a rapidly changing world. Enthusiastically embracing these tools can propel your outreach efforts into new realms of effectiveness and impact, illustrating that faith, paired with innovation, can move mountains and transcend borders in the digital age.

* * *

Now, pause for a moment and reflect. Are we fully utilizing the digital tools at our disposal? Are we transforming our ministries with the innovation and efficiency that technology offers? The call to integrate technology into our mission is clear, urging us to unlock our potential and live out our calling in the digital age.

This is an invitation to empower, to innovate, and to lead with faith at the forefront of our efforts. By embracing technology, we not only enhance our outreach but also fortify our commitment to serve, to educate, and to inspire. The question now is not whether we can afford to leverage technology, but whether we can afford not to.

Thus, as we stand on the brink of possibilities, let us move forward with confidence and faith. Technology is more than just a tool; it's a catalyst for transformation, a way to amplify our message and mission across the globe. Together, empowered by the digital age, we can achieve sustainability, reach hearts, and change lives in ways we never thought possible.

Cultivating Corporate Partnerships

Synergistic partnerships with corporations present substantial opportunities. Not only do they provide a new source of revenue, but they also bring valuable resources and expertise to the table. In today's world, Corporate Social Responsibility (CSR) plays an increasingly significant role in business strategies, with companies recognizing the value of giving back to communities and aligning themselves with causes that resonate with their values.

By strategically identifying potential corporate partners, we can tap into their resources and expertise to amplify our mission. This requires a proactive approach, where we reach out to businesses whose values align with ours and propose mutually beneficial partnerships.

Possible avenues for collaboration include cause-related marketing campaigns, event sponsorships, employee volunteer programs, and in-kind donations. These partnerships can not only provide vital financial support but also bring new networks of potential supporters to our cause.

However, it's important to approach these partnerships with a clear and well-defined proposition. Showing how our mission can align with their business objectives and values will make the partnership more attractive to corporations. Additionally, maintaining strong communication and demonstrating the impact of their contributions will keep the relationship thriving for years to come.

The Power of Storytelling

Finally, one of the most impactful ways to engage and inspire others is through the power of storytelling. As human beings, we are inherently drawn to narratives that connect with our emotions and experiences. And as people of faith, we have a wealth of powerful stories to share.

Whether it's sharing personal testimonies of transformation or highlighting the impact of our organization's work in someone's life, storytelling allows us to connect with others on a deeper level. By humanizing our message, we can inspire empathy and understanding, fostering a sense of community and support for our cause.

In today's digital era, storytelling has also evolved to include various mediums such as videos, social media posts, and blogs. Leveraging these platforms to share stories of hope and transformation can reach a wider audience and create a stronger impact.

As we continue to navigate the ever-changing landscape of faith-based outreach, it's important to stay current and adaptable. By utilizing technology, seeking strategic partnerships, and harnessing the power of storytelling, we can continue to spread our message of love, hope, and transformation to individuals around the world.

Nurturing an Entrepreneurial Culture

In the vibrant tapestry of today's non-profit landscape, how can we nurture an entrepreneurial culture that not only survives but thrives? This question isn't just rhetoric; it's a clarion call for leaders who dare to dream big and act boldly. Institutionalizing an entrepreneurial culture within non-profits isn't just beneficial—it's imperative for fostering agility and a willingness to innovate.

Nurturing an entrepreneurial culture is about creating an environment where creativity flourishes, where every team member feels empowered to bring forward innovative ideas, and where taking calculated risks is not just accepted but encouraged.

Imagine a world where non-profits are not just keeping pace but setting the tempo for change and impact. This is the power of an entrepreneurial culture.

Question for Thought: Are we fully unleashing the potential within our teams? Are we creating spaces where the spirit of entrepreneurship can soar, bringing with it fresh perspectives and groundbreaking solutions? The journey towards cultivating this culture is filled with challenges, yes, but also with unparalleled opportunities to empower, to innovate, and to transform.

Repetition isn't just a technique; it's our mantra.

> Empower
>
> Innovate
>
> Transform...

These aren't just words, they're the pillars upon which the future of non-profit organizations rests. By repeating these ideas, we reinforce not just the message but the commitment to live out these values in every action we take.

Power words like "empower," "unlock your potential," and "live out your calling" are not merely motivational tools; they're beacons that guide us towards realizing our full potential. They evoke strong emotions and inspire us to take action, to make a difference, and to be the change we wish to see in the world.

Now, ask yourself, are we ready to take this leap? Are we prepared to foster an entrepreneurial spirit that propels our mission forward? This isn't just about adopting new strategies; it's about embodying a mindset that embraces change, champions innovation, and pursues sustainability with unwavering faith and determination.

This is our moment to shine, to show the world that non-profits can be both mission-driven and innovative. It's our time to unlock the doors of possibility, to empower our teams, and to live out our calling in ways that resonate deeply with both our values and the needs of those we serve.

. . .

The path to nurturing an entrepreneurial culture is paved with commitment, creativity, and courage. Are you ready to walk this path, to unlock your potential, and to inspire others to do the same? Together, with faith as our guide, we can transform challenges into opportunities, turning our visions into realities. The future awaits, and it's brighter than we can imagine.

Nurturing an Entrepreneurial Culture can be achieved through:

- **Leadership Commitment:** Senior leaders must champion innovation, modeling the risk-taking and learning-oriented mindset required for entrepreneurial ventures.

- **Staff Empowerment:** Encouraging and supporting staff to pursue new ideas and initiatives fosters an organizational environment that embraces change and growth.

- **Strategic Planning:** Incorporating sustainability and innovation goals into the organization's strategic plan provides a clear roadmap that aligns efforts towards a common vision.

- **Open Communication:** Creating a culture of open communication and transparency allows for the exchange of ideas, feedback, and collaboration among team members.

- **Embracing Failure as a Learning Opportunity:** In an entrepreneurial culture, failure is not seen as a setback but rather as a chance to learn, pivot, and grow. This mindset encourages risk-taking and iteration towards success.

- **Collaboration and Partnerships:** Building strategic partnerships with other organizations, businesses, or individuals can bring new perspectives, resources, and support to further the organization's mission.

- **Continuous Learning:** Investing in continuous learning opportunities for staff ensures that they are equipped with the skills and knowledge needed to innovate and drive the organization forward.

Nurturing an entrepreneurial culture requires a collective effort from all team members. By embracing change, taking risks, and fostering a learning-oriented mindset, we can create an environment that not only survives but thrives in today's fast-paced world.

Case Studies in Non-Profit Innovation

Real-world examples can serve as touchstones for the application of social entrepreneurship in non-profits. These case studies demonstrate how organizations have successfully embraced an entrepreneurial mindset to drive their impact and achieve sustainability. Let's explore some of them:

- **The Mobile Library Initiative**: In the heart of rural Africa, where access to books and educational materials is a significant challenge, the Mobile Library Initiative has revolutionized learning. By converting old vans into mobile libraries, stocked with books, e-readers, and internet-accessible computers, they're bringing education directly to remote communities. This innovative approach has increased literacy rates and has empowered children and adults with the tools for self-education, opening doors to personal and community development that once seemed firmly shut.

- **The Solar Water Farms**: Facing the acute challenge of clean water scarcity in arid regions, The Solar Water Farms have implemented a groundbreaking solution. Utilizing desalination technology powered by renewable solar energy, they're able to produce clean, safe drinking water for communities that have suffered from severe water-related problems. This not only improves health outcomes by reducing waterborne diseases but also frees up significant time for education and economic activities, particularly for women and girls who primarily bear the burden of water collection.

- **Digital Skills for the Homeless**: In an era where digital literacy is paramount, a forward-thinking non-profit in urban centers across the United States has launched a program to teach digital skills to the homeless population. Through access to computers and personalized training, participants gain vital skills needed for modern employment opportunities. More than just a training program, it's a bridge to stability—

facilitating job searches, housing applications, and social connections. This initiative not only tackles homelessness but equips individuals with the confidence and tools to thrive in the digital age.

- **Kiva**: With a mission to alleviate poverty through Microfinance, Kiva has used an innovative peer-to-peer lending platform to connect lenders and borrowers worldwide, providing opportunities for financial empowerment. By leveraging technology and a community-driven approach, Kiva has transformed traditional lending models and empowered individuals to break the cycle of poverty.

- **Teach for All**: This global network of independent non-profits is transforming education by recruiting, training, and supporting talented teachers to address educational inequities and create positive change in their communities. By fostering a culture of innovation and collaboration, Teach for All is setting a new standard for education and inspiring future generations to become leaders in their communities.

These case studies demonstrate the incredible power of innovative thinking in the non-profit sector. By addressing education, environmental sustainability, and social inequality, these initiatives are making tangible differences in their communities. The success of these projects lies not just in their novel approaches but in their ability to harness technology and human capital for the greater good. They stand as inspiring examples for non-profits worldwide to think creatively in solving complex social issues.

Overcoming Challenges and Risks

In the exhilarating quest of social entrepreneurship within non-profits, the road is undoubtedly paved with both opportunities and challenges. Have you ever stopped to consider the sheer magnitude of impact you could have, not just in your community, but in the world? It's a thought that ignites the soul, isn't it? Yet, as we stand on the precipice of change, ready to leap into the unknown, it's imperative to acknowledge that this path is not without obstacles.

But what are these challenges, and more importantly, how do we overcome them? The hurdles range from securing consistent funding to navigating regulatory landscapes and everything in between. These risks are real, but should they deter us? Absolutely not. Instead, they serve as a call to action—a reminder that with great faith and determination, any obstacle can be overcome.

In the face of adversity, where do we find the strength to persevere? The answer lies within, driven by the belief that our work is not merely a job but a calling. This belief empowers us to innovate, to strategize, and to forge ahead with unwavering conviction, even when the road gets tough.

Why, then, do we choose to walk this path? The answer is simple yet profound. We are called to serve, to empower, and to make a difference. This calling is not for the faint-hearted; it requires courage, resilience, and, above all, faith. Faith that our efforts will bear fruit, faith in the power of innovation, and faith that, together, we can overcome any challenge that comes our way.

Now, imagine for a moment, the potential that lies within

each of us to effect change. Is it not awe-inspiring? Think of the lives that could be transformed through our collective efforts. This vision, however ambitious, is achievable. But it demands that we step out in faith, armed with a strategy and a heart full of purpose.

The road ahead is indeed fraught with risks and uncertainties, but it's also brimming with possibilities. Are we prepared to face these challenges head-on? Are we ready to unlock our potential, to live out our calling, and to leave an indelible mark on the world? The answer must be a resounding yes.

With each step forward, we embody the essence of social entrepreneurship. We become beacons of hope in a world in desperate need of healing. This is not just our mission; it's our ministry. Together, empowered by faith and driven by a shared vision, we can transform obstacles into steppingstones, leading the way to a brighter, more sustainable future.

In conclusion, the narratives of innovation, resilience, and impact shared in this chapter underscore a profound truth: non-profit organizations are not just surviving; they are thriving by adapting to change and confronting challenges head-on. The examples of The Mully Children's Home, The Solar Water Farms, Digital Skills Training, Kiva, and Teach for All, and more... illustrate vividly how non-profits can sustain their mission by leveraging technology, engaging communities, and fostering partnerships to amplify their impact.

The key to sustainability lies not merely in securing funds or navigating regulations but in cultivating a mindset of adaptability, collaboration, and relentless pursuit of mission-driven goals. It's about creating a legacy of positive change that outlives us, built on the foundations of innovation, equity, and social responsibility.

As we forge ahead, our collective efforts in the non-profit sector will serve as a beacon of hope and a testament to the indomitable human spirit's capacity to enact meaningful change. The road ahead is replete with opportunities to redefine the future, reshape our communities, and reaffirm our unwavering commitment to serve humanity. Together, we stand on the cusp of a new era in non-profit sustainability, where our actions today will pave the way for a more equitable, just, and vibrant world tomorrow.

May I Introduce You to Jesus?

Are you feeling lost, searching for a purpose in life? Do you feel that something is missing, and you are not sure what it is? Do you want to know more about Jesus and the Bible? If yes, then you are in the right place. In this chapter, we will explore what a relationship with Jesus can mean for your life and eternity. The Bible says that when we come to Jesus, we receive spiritual rebirth, the forgiveness of sins, and eternal life. Let's talk about it.

The Biblical Basis for Coming to Jesus

God has provided us with precise instructions on how to come to Him through His Word, the Bible. Our first step is acknowledging our sins. Romans 3:23 says,

> *"For all have sinned and fall short of the glory of God."*

Therefore, we must recognize that we cannot save

ourselves with our own efforts. However, Jesus can save us, and we must believe in Him to receive salvation.

Acceptance and belief in His Word affect our lives in many ways. John 1:12 says,

> "Yet to all who did receive him, to those who believed in his name, he gave the right to become children of God."

By accepting Jesus into our lives, we gain the privilege of being God's children, and this changes our identity. We will have a new purpose in life and a new perspective on our struggles. We will experience forgiveness, acceptance, divine love, and the joy of living for God daily.

The Cross of Calvary reveals the ultimate sacrifice of Jesus Christ for our sins. Romans 5:8 says,

> "But God demonstrates his love for us in this: While we were still sinners, Christ died for us."

Jesus paid the price for our sins, and we can receive forgiveness and salvation through Him. It is through His death and resurrection that we can come to the Father and receive the Holy Spirit.

As humans, we all have our shortcomings and faults. No one is perfect, and that's why we need Jesus in our lives. Romans 6:23 states,

> "For the wages of sin is death; but the gift of God is eternal life through Jesus Christ our Lord."

It's a beautiful thing to know that there's a way out of the darkness, and that's through Jesus Christ. Its not an easy decision to make, but its a crucial one that we all must make if we want to experience true freedom and life. So, if you're feeling lost and hopeless today, know that there's hope in Jesus. He's waiting with open arms to welcome you into His love and grace.

Praying a prayer of salvation is a simple and powerful step toward salvation. We must confess our faith and ask for forgiveness of our sins. Romans 10:9 says,

> *"If you declare with your mouth, Jesus is Lord, and believe in your heart that God raised him from the dead, you will be saved."*

The following is a simple prayer guide:

Dear Lord Jesus,

I know that I am a sinner and that I cannot save myself. I believe that you died on the Cross for my sins and that you rose again. Please forgive me of my sins and come into my heart. Right now, I confess and receive You as my Lord and Savior. Thank you for giving me eternal life. In Jesus' name, Amen.

What Now?

Congratulations on your decision to follow Jesus Christ and join the family of God! You are no longer alone in your journey of faith. It's exciting to think about the wonderful things God has in store for you as you grow and mature in Him. Whether you are new to Christianity or have walked with the Lord for a while, this guide will help you navigate the ups and downs of your faith journey.

Being a part of the Family of God is a rich and rewarding experience that comes with responsibilities and opportunities. Now that you have received salvation, you have the privilege of being called a child of God. The concept of having a personal relationship with Jesus Christ must be taken seriously, as it is an ongoing process if one is to continuously grow in their faith.

Daily Prayer

The first step is to understand the power of prayer. Prayer is a conversation with God that helps establish and strengthen an intimate relationship with Him. Cultivate the habit of prayer by setting aside a specific time each day to talk with God. One of the most important components of prayer is learning how to listen to what God is trying to say. Many people think that prayer is constantly talking to God. May I encourage you that prayer is one part talking and two parts listening. Just look in the mirror; we all have one mouth and two ears.

Praying daily is a wonderful way to connect with God's heart and deepen your relationship with Him. It allows for open communication so that you can share your thoughts, feelings, and aspirations with Him. You may also take this time to thank Him for your blessings and ask for His guidance in making decisions. With each prayer, you build a stronger connection with God and can find peace knowing that He is always there to listen and support you.

Throughout the years, many people have asked me,

"How can I hear God's voice?"

My answer to them has consistently been,

"If we sit in His presence, we can learn His voice."

God speaks to everyone differently. He wants to have an

active relationship "with you, and the best way to do this is through communication. One of the ways that God has communicated to us is through His Word.

Daily Bible Reading

Reading the Bible is an incredible way to receive guidance on God's will for your life. The Bible contains gems of wisdom and encouragement that can help us navigate the twists and turns of life. Whether we're facing a tough decision, feeling lost or simply seeking direction, the Bible is a faithful companion that provides solid, reliable advice. What's more, the Bible is a gift that strengthens our relationship with God. Through reading its pages, we can learn about His character, understand His love and gain a deeper appreciation of His goodness. Reading the Bible isn't just about finding direction - its about drawing closer to the One who created us and has a hope-filled plan for our lives.

To grow in faith and knowledge, one must engage in daily bible reading and study. The Bible is the guidebook that reveals who God is, what He has done, and what He expects of us. In addition to personal bible reading, its important to receive sound teaching through fellowship with other believers. It's helpful to attend small groups, Sunday services, and listen to online messages. With practice, the things you learn will become deeply rooted in your heart and transform your life.

Christian Friends

Finding Christian friends is also essential to your growth in faith. When you're immersed in a community of believers, you have the opportunity to build deep, authentic relationships. These relationships build support and accountability, which will help you stay on the right path. Connecting with a church community is vital to your spiritual growth. A church provides a place where you can worship God in community, hear the Word preached, and serve the body of Christ.

Being part of a church provides not only solid teaching but a community of like-minded believers that share a common faith. There is nothing quite like experiencing the joy of fellowship with others who are seeking to grow in their relationship with God. You'll find people who come from all walks of life, with different backgrounds and experiences but united in a common goal - to know and love God more deeply. As you sit under the teaching of pastors and teachers, you'll discover a depth to your faith that you never thought possible. Through worship, prayer, and study of the Bible, you'll feel your heart expanding with an overwhelming sense of gratitude and thankfulness for all that God is doing in your life. Truly, belonging to a church is an experience that is both fulfilling and life-changing.

Developing a Servants Heart

Putting your learning into practice through the practical application of your faith is an important step in growth. Serving others is one way to do so. Jesus spent His life serving others and has called us to do the same. Jesus' example reminds us that we need to get outside of our comfort zones and bless others with our time, energy, and resources. Volunteer at church, donate to a charity, or work in your community. With time, as you serve and bless others, you'll find that God is guiding and shaping you into a better version of yourself.

Living Grateful

Living a life that is grateful, faithful, and holy is truly a blessing. As we honor God in all areas of our lives, we can't help but feel an overwhelming sense of joy and fulfillment. It's not always the easiest path to take, but when we choose to put our trust in Him and seek His will for our lives, we can rest assured that we are on the right track. When we live with gratitude in our hearts, we begin to see the world in a different light, and our relationships with others are strengthened. Ultimately, living a life that honors God is the best decision we can make, and we can trust that He will guide us every step of the way.

Pride and gratitude cannot co-exist. Rejoicing in the blessings of salvation is the ultimate goal of every Christian. It's easy to get bogged down in day-to-day challenges that we forget to celebrate the victory we have in Jesus. To celebrate the goodness of God, it's essential to practice gratitude. Remember that your salvation is a free gift from God that you didn't deserve, and nothing you do can take it away. Celebrate divine love, mercy, and grace by sharing joyful testimonies with others. Encourage others with your story and how God has changed your life.

Welcome to the Family!

About the Author

For more information on Dr. Jonathan Vorce just go to
www.about.me/jonathanvorce

Affordable | Accessible | Accredited | Online

Dr. Vorce is the Chancellor of Covenant University, Inc. Degrees range from first year through Ph.D.

More information is available on our website:
www.covenantuniversityonline.com

Also by Jonathan & Donna Vorce

Presence Driven

Hosting the Holy Ghost

Christian Leadership

Building Successful Ministry

Shepherding in the 21st Century

Kingdom Economics

Divine Authority

The Ministry of Presence (Chaplaincy)

All books may be ordered on Amazon.com and most online places where books are sold.

www.ingramcontent.com/pod-product-compliance
Lightning Source LLC
Chambersburg PA
CBHW052300220526
45471CB00001B/420